Twayne's United States Authors Series

Sylvia E. Bowman, Editor

INDIANA UNIVERSITY

John Berryman

JOHN BERRYMAN

Tom Berthiaume

JOHN BERRYMAN

By J. M. Linebarger
North Texas State University

 244

Twayne Publishers, Inc. :: New York

Library of Congress Cataloging in Publication Data

Linebarger, J   M
    John Berryman.

    (Twayne's United States authors series, TUSAS 244)
    Bibliography: p.
    1.   Berryman, John, 1914-1972.
PS3503.E744Z76   811'.5'4   73-17367
ISBN 0-8057-0054-4

FOR LILLIAN

Preface

The purposes of this study of John Berryman are those of the Twayne Series generally: to introduce a writer to the common reader, to teachers, to students, to scholars. The methods used are those of paraphrase and explication combined with a broader approach that includes pertinent background information and secondary materials but does not, I hope, lean unnecessarily on them. Professional critics of literature may find this examination of Berryman's work to be simplistic, but I cannot honestly claim that the study could have been more perceptive if my audience had been limited to them. Above all my purpose is to be clear.

The study attempts to give a proper emphasis to Berryman's poetry, his most important achievement. His two short stories were published in the best places and received high praise, and his critical biography of Stephen Crane is considered a useful work on that writer. But his poetry will determine Berryman's place in literature, for it is infused with a personal intensity that, in his criticism, becomes enthusiasm and tends to distort his critical intelligence. His poems, especially the later ones called the Dream Songs, are now finding a relatively large audience among readers both of a conservative and of a radical bent—the Academics and the Beats, the Dead-men and the Alive, or the Houyhnhnms and the Yahoos, depending upon the reader's own prejudices.

The first chapter surveys Berryman's life and career; it includes much biographical detail that becomes relevant to a discussion of the poetry. The ensuing chapters are arranged chronologically, loosely dividing Berryman's poetic career into four periods. The early period includes the collections "Twenty Poems" (1940), *Poems* (1942), and *The Dispossessed* (1948). The early poetry was often influenced by Yeats and Auden, but it also suggested the basic themes and subjects that were to recur throughout Berryman's career.

Berryman's Sonnets (written in 1947) and *Homage to Mistress Bradstreet* (1953) belong to a transitional period, a time when Berryman had clearly escaped the influence of Yeats and Auden and had found voices of his own.

But the poet seems to have been uncertain of his direction until about 1955, when he began to write *Dream Songs*. They are discussed in Chapter Four, primarily by examining their attitudes toward Berryman's characteristic subjects: sociopolitical concerns, the nature of art and poetry, religion, love, psychological disorder, ahp the overwhelming sense of loss that dominates Berryman's poetry from early to late. Chapter Five examines Berryman's last two volumes of poetry, *Love & Fame* (1970) and *Delusions, etc.* (1972), and his uncompleted novel *Recovery* (1973). The approach to these volumes tends more to paraphrase and summary, for Berryman's late work is comparatively direct, explicit, and obviously autobiographical. Chapter Six, the conclusion, argues first that Berryman's Dream Songs combine certain qualities of Academic and Beat poetry — the two dominant trends in American poetry since World War II — and then that these poems assure Berryman a place alongside the best poets of his generation.

The reason for the obtrusive documentation in Chapter One is that I am trying not to add to the errors of biographical fact that accumulate around any writer who is just coming into the awareness of a large public; but no doubt I have unknowingly made such contributions at one point or another. The poet himself was not an unimpeachable source of biographical information. He was deeply interested in the lives of the writers he was enthusiastic about—Shakespeare and Stephen Crane, for example—but he was sometimes reticent about his own, or humorously exaggerative, or breezily unconcerned. He once wrote in reply to a biographical question, "Who cares?" But in fairness I must say that John Berryman was very helpful, answering most of my questions, including several that were petty, impertinent, or irrelevant. He was properly concerned that his work, taken together, not be misread simply as a straightforward and factual autobiography.

A traditional bow is owed to many friends, students, and colleagues without whose aid such a study as this would surely have been completed, but not by me. Thanks go to Jim Baird, Jere Bass, William Belcher, Jefferson Berryman, Louise Boyd, Mary Buckalew, Jim Culpepper, Tony Damico, James Davidson,

Lyle Domina, Howard L. Ford, Priscilla Glenn, Paula Grubb, Thomas Hall, Helen Hanicak, Thomas S. Harllee, Sam H. Henderson, David B. Kesterson, J. F. Kobler, Joe Lyle, Joseph M. Logue, Robert A. Lopez, Charles B. Martin, Barbara A. McDaniel, Michael Mesic, Richard B. Sale, Arthur M. Sampley, L. Robert Stevens, James T. F. Tanner, Anne Tims, and Lester Wittenberg, Jr. I gratefully acknowledge the leave granted by the Board of Regents of North Texas State University, A.M. Willis, Jr., Chairman. And I thank those who recommended me for the leave; Ernest S. Clifton, Chairman of the Department of English; and the Committee on Faculty Development Leave, Miles E. Anderson, Chairman. My thanks go also to the North Texas Faculty Research Committee, Robert B. Toulouse, Chairman, and Robert C. Sherman, Executive Secretary. Giles Mitchell and Eugene P. Wright read the manuscript and made many helpful suggestions; I am especially indebted to them.

Anyone who writes a study of this sort hopes that it will lead the reader to a closer examination and finer appreciation of the poet's work. Most of Berryman's poetry is readily available in recent editions; the reader will find it helpful at points to refer to that poetry directly, for Berryman's present publishers have permitted me to quote no poem in its entirety and no more than five hundred lines of the poetry altogether. The unavoidable result is more paraphrasing and fewer direct quotations than I would prefer. But I hope also that this study can stand by itself as an introduction to one of the finest and most interesting poets of our time.

J. M. LINEBARGER

North Texas State University

Acknowledgments

Berryman's Sonnets, by John Berryman. Copyright © 1952, 1967 by John Berryman; published by Farrar, Straus & Giroux. Reprinted with the permission of Farrar, Straus & Giroux, Inc.

"Berryman's Sonnets: Tradition and the Individual Talent," by J. M. Linebarger; published by *Concerning Poetry.* Copyright © 1973. Reprinted with the permission of the editors of *Concerning Poetry.*

Delusions, etc., by John Berryman. Copyright © 1969, 1971 by John Berryman, Copyright © 1972 by the Estate of John Berryman; published by Farrar, Straus & Giroux.

The Dream Songs, by John Berryman. Copyright © 1959, 1962, 1963, 1964, 1965, 1966, 1967, 1968, 1969 by John Berryman; published by Farrar, Straus & Giroux. Reprinted with the permission of Farrar, Straus & Giroux, Inc.

The Harvard Advocate, CIII (Spring 1969). Copyright 1969 by the Editors and Trustees of *The Harvard Advocate.*

Homage to Mistress Bradstreet, by John Berryman. Copyright © 1956 by John Berryman; published by Farrar, Straus & Giroux. Reprinted with the permission of Farrar, Straus & Giroux, Inc.

John Berryman, by William J. Martz, University of Minnesota Pamphlets on American Writers No. 85. University of Minnesota Press, Minneapolis. Copyright © 1969 by the University of Minnesota.

Contents

Chronology

1914- 1925	John Berryman born October 25, 1914, McAlester, Oklahoma; named John Allyn Smith, after his father. Spends childhood in McAlester and other Oklahoma towns. Brother, Jefferson, born 1919. Family moves to Tampa, Florida.
1926- 1927	Father commits suicide, 1926. Family moves to Gloucester, Massachusetts; then to Jackson Heights, Queens, New York. Mother marries John Angus McAlpin Berryman, who legally adopts John and Jefferson. Poet's name becomes John Allyn McAlpin Berryman.
1928- 1932	Attends South Kent School in Connecticut. Leaves before senior year to enter Columbia College.
1932- 1936	Attends Columbia. Studies literature and philosophy. Becomes friends with Mark Van Doren and, inspired by him, decides to become a poet. Begins to publish poetry in 1935. After failing a course, is expelled for one semester, but returns to make Phi Beta Kappa. Bachelor of Arts degree, spring 1936. Awarded Kellett Fellowship by Columbia.
1936- 1938	Attends Clare College, Cambridge. Has serious love affair. Travels several times to the Continent. Meets William Butler Yeats, Dylan Thomas, and W. H. Auden. Selected as Oldham Shakespeare Scholar for 1937. Receives Bachelor of Arts degree, spring 1938.
1938- 1939	Lives in New York City; becomes friends with Delmore Schwartz.
1939- 1940	Begins teaching career as an instructor in English, Wayne University, Detroit. "Twenty Poems" published in *Five Young American Poets* (1940).

1940- 1943	Briggs-Copeland Instructor in Composition at Harvard. Publishes *Poems* (1942). Marries first wife, Eileen Patricia Mulligan, October 24, 1942.
1943- 1951	Intermittently a fellow and an instructor in creative writing at Princeton. Receives many prizes and awards. In 1947, engages in an adulterous love affair and begins to undergo psychoanalysis, but continues to teach and to write. *Berryman's Sonnets* (written in 1947, published 1967); poems recorded for Library of Congress, 1948; *Homage to Mistress Bradstreet* begun *ca.* 1948; *The Dispossessed* (poetry) published 1948; *Ezra Pound: Selected Poems* (edited by Berryman) published 1949. *Stephen Crane* (critical biography) published 1950.
1951- 1952	Elliston Lecturer in Poetry at the University of Cincinnati. Writes introduction to an edition of Matthew Gregory Lewis's *The Monk* (1952).
1952- 1953	Guggenheim Fellowship. Travels to Europe. Separation from Eileen, 1953. *Homage to Mistress Bradstreet* (poem) published 1953.
1954	Teaches poetry at the State University of Iowa, spring; teaches at Harvard, summer. In October becomes a lecturer in the humanities program at the University of Minnesota, where he taught until the time of his death.
ca. 1955	Begins to write *Dream Songs*.
1956	Divorced from Eileen. Marries Ann Levine.
1957	Awarded the Harriet Monroe Poetry Prize and a *Partisan Review* fellowship. Makes a two-month trip to India for the State Department. Son, Paul, born.
1958	Publishes *His Thought Made Pockets & The Plane Buckt* (poetry).
1959	Divorced from Ann. Awarded the Brandeis University Creative Arts Award.
1960	Visiting professor, University of California at Berkeley. Edits Thomas Nashe's *Unfortunate Traveller*. Writes (with Ralph Ross and Allen Tate) *The Arts of Reading* (anthology with commentary).
1961	Marries Kathleen ("Kate") Donahue. Visiting professor, Indiana University.
1962- 1963	Visiting professor, Brown University. Daughter, Martha (called "Twissy"), born.

1964   Awarded honorary Master of Arts degree by Cambridge. Publication of *77 Dream Songs* (poetry).

1965   Awarded Pulitzer Prize (for *77 Dream Songs*). Elected to National Institute of Arts and Letters.

1966
1967   Awarded second Guggenheim fellowship, Ingram Merrill Foundation grant, and sabbatical leave from Minnesota. Spends the school year 1966-67 in Ireland, working primarily on new Dream Songs. Returns to New York City for ten days during the spring of 1967 to accept a fellowship from the Academy of American Poets. Receives $10,000 award from the National Endowment for the Arts. *Berryman's Sonnets* and *Short Poems* published.

1968   *His Toy, His Dream, His Rest* (a continuation of *77 Dream Songs*) published.

1969   *His Toy, His Dream, His Rest* wins the National Book Award and a share of the Bollingen Prize. *The Dream Songs* (combined edition) published. Named a Regents' Professor at the University of Minnesota.

1970   *Love & Fame* (poetry) published.

1971   Awarded a Doctor of Letters degree by Drake University. Sarah Rebecca, daughter, is born.

1972   Commits suicide, January 7. *Delusions, etc.* (poetry) published posthumously.

1973   *Recovery* (novel) published.

CHAPTER *1*

Biographical and Introductory

JOHN Berryman wrote and published poetry regularly from 1935 to 1972, and his literary reputation varied considerably during that time. In the 1940's, he was considered a rising young poet of restrained and carefully formed academic verse. Three slim collections of it had been published by 1948, and four of these early poems were anthologized in Louis Untermeyer's *Modern American Poetry* (1950). But during the 1950's Berryman's promise was not realized. His long poem *Homage to Mistress Bradstreet* (1953)[1] had a readership limited largely to fellow poets and writers, and it baffled many of them, including some who praised the poem highly. The eleven poems of *His Thought Made Pockets & the Plane Buckt* (1958)[2] were uneven and represented no advance beyond the earlier works. With the exception of *Homage,* which found its way into Conrad Aiken's *Twentieth-Century American Poetry* (1963), little of Berryman's verse was included in the standard anthologies of the 1950's and early 1960's, one indication of a declining reputation. There was none of it in Oscar Williams's *Pocket Book of Modern Verse* (1954), George P. Elliott's *Modern American Poets* (1956), or Chad Walsh's *Today's Poets* (1964).

But in 1964, when he was fifty, Berryman published *77 Dream Songs,* which won a Pulitzer Prize and created a sensation in the literary world. Because of the stir the Songs caused, several earlier works were reprinted—or, in the case of *Berryman's Sonnets* (1967),[3] printed for the first time. Berryman became, as he said, "hot as a pistol."[4] *His Toy, His Dream, His Rest* (1968), a final installment of Dream Songs, won the National Book Award and a share of the Bollingen Prize. *The Dream Songs* (1969),[5] a combined edition of *77 Dream Songs* and *His Toy, His Dream, His Rest,* is one of the few volumes of poetry to become a book-club selection. An indication of the poet's increasing popularity is his inclusion in recent anthologies—in Mark Strand's *Contemporary American Poets* (1969) and in A. Poulin's *Contemporary American Poetry* (1971). Generally, the accepted view at present is that Berryman is in the first rank of modern American poets.

I *The Suicide of His Father*

To say that we must know something of a poet's life in order to understand his work is a cliché, but in Berryman's case it is also a fact. Even in his early poetry there are veiled allusions that require biographical information, and Berryman's subject increasingly became himself. He always insisted that he did not write poetic autobiography, and certainly his poetry is more than just a factual recounting of the events of his life—it is an imaginative recreation of them. Following recent trends in poetry, his later works—*The Dream Songs, Love & Fame,* and *Delusions, etc.*[6] are essentially autobiographical.

The poet was born in McAlester, Oklahoma, on October 25, 1914. A first son, he was named after his father, John Allyn Smith. (Some confusion exists about the poet's name.[7] The surname "Berryman" is one that he assumed when, as a teenager, he was legally adopted by John Angus McAlpin Berryman; the poet's full name then became John Allyn McAlpin Berryman.) The poet's father was a banker in McAlester; his mother, Martha (Little) Smith, a schoolteacher. The "parents had separately and by chance migrated from farther east,"[8] had met while "living in the same boarding house," and had married, the poet says, because "they were the only people who could read and write for hundreds of miles around. . . ."[9] Perhaps they were also attracted to each other because both were Roman Catholics in a heavily Protestant section of the country. A second son, Jefferson, was born in 1919[10].

In most ways John's early boyhood in McAlester and in other small Oklahoma towns seems to have been fairly normal. He suffered the usual childhood diseases (one of which left him partially deaf), read heavily, and enjoyed cowboy movies. But

when he was ten the family moved to Tampa, Florida, where his mother and father had severe marital difficulties. His father, fearing that his wife was about to leave him, repeatedly threatened to drown himself and John with him. Lack of money was not the problem; in fact, young John had an allowance of $25 a week, all of which he spent on his stamp collection. His relationship with each of his parents was, moreover, close. His father, a captain in the National Guard, even took the boy with him occasionally when he went on maneuvers to Fort Sill, Oklahoma, as well as on hunting and fishing trips.[11]

But on June 26, 1926, at a vacation house across the bay from Tampa, John's father killed himself with a pistol. His father's suicide was one of the most significant events in the poet's life. In his fifties the poet said that he still suffered "from an exaggerated case of what Freud calls 'infantile amnesia,' "[12] but his poetry refers often to his father's death and to its effects on him. His obsession with it, and with his own anticipated suicide, was his most persistent idea.

Within a year after his father's death, John began his literary career by writing half of a science-fiction novel which was probably influenced by Jules Verne since it describes a journey beneath the sea ("Shirley & Auden," *Love & Fame,*7). Although he had briefly dreamed of being an archaeologist (Dream Song 30), he once recalled that he "always wanted to be a writer."[13]

II *Education*

After the father's death the family moved first to Gloucester, Massachusetts, and then to Jackson Heights, Queens, New York.[14] The poet's mother married John Angus McAlpin Berryman, a Wall Street banker and a man "somewhat older" than she.[15] In Queens, John attended P.S. 69 "for some years," he says[16]; but it seems that he was in school there only during the school year 1927-28; for, in the fall of 1928, "after having passed the entrance examinations with some brilliance,"[17] he entered South Kent School in Connecticut. "South Kent was, in John's later words, 'very muscular,' that is, devoted to athletics, and very high-church Episcopalian."[18] Berryman "took part in athletics . . . only to the extent that he had to. . . . Even then he had some trouble with his eyes which made it difficult for him to be expert in any athletic endeavor."[19] "He was much bullied there, had many fights—usually with stand-off results—. . . and rebelled because he was an intellectual and the school, as he saw it, was not sympathetic to intellectuals."[20] Curiously, Berryman never led the school academically, but a former classmate commented in 1970, "I think he could have done so any time he wanted to. . . . [Recently] he told me that he had deliberately 'fudged' a course or two . . . so that somebody else would stay ahead of him."[21] Berryman found two of the masters at South Kent to be "stimulating"[22] and "sympathetic to him personally,"[23] but "by the end of his Fifth Form year (11th grade) [he] had exhausted all the possibilities of South Kent academically, and he left the year before the rest of the class to go to Columbia. He returned in June of 1933 to graduate technically with the class of 1933 and receive his diploma."[24]

At Columbia, Berryman determinedly set out to become accepted by his peers. He tells us in "In & Out" (*Love & Fame,* 24), that he had been a miserable loner at South Kent, but he claims to have learned the names of most of his five hundred Columbia classmates within a month after enrolling there—even the names of the commuters, who were flattered just to be recognized on campus. He began to feel that he belonged, and he viewed his classmates and himself as cosmopolites and equals. He wore the unofficial Columbia uniform of the time (which included white buckskin shoes that were scuffed to a dirty gray), and he attended the usual round of social activities for undergraduates, making a name for himself as an energetic and imaginative dancer ("My Special Fate," *Love & Fame,* 12).

He rowed on the freshman crew team and, in track, ran the quarter-mile and half-mile—"not very rapidly," he admitted, "but fast enough to win my numerals."[25] He became involved in campus politics, entering the race for the vice-presidency of his class, but he lost the election by only five votes to a fraternity boy who had attended Kent School ("Shirley & Auden," *Love & Fame,* 7), a defeat that must have been doubly painful because Kent and South Kent were rivals. He made friends with classmates, Barnard girls, "townies," football players, and most importantly, with Mark Van Doren, "the teacher who inspired him. . . , all of whose courses he took."[26]

As Berryman recalled their relationship, he was probably inaccurate in diction but exact in conveying the warmth of the friendship: "I became friends with him and I called him 'Sir'—a habit I had picked up at prep school. . . . So I called Mark, 'Sir'; so he said, 'If you call me "sir" once more I'll kick you. . . .' I was very touched by this, so I didn't call him 'sir' anymore."[27] Mark Van Doren recalls that "as a student [Berryman] was high-strung, nervous, intense, devoted to his friends, morally indignant on frequent occasions, beautifully relaxed on other occasions just as frequent, sensible at best, and always witty; though he took things hard, and sometimes seemed to be composed of nothing but bristles and points."[28]

Berryman's statements about the importance of Van Doren to his development as a writer are unequivocal: ". . . I never imagined being a poet, until I reviewed Mark Van Doren's book, *A Winter Diary* [1935]. . . ."[29] Berryman had begun to write poetry before 1935. He says that he was "about nineteen" when he wrote four sonnets for his mother;[30] but it was the stimulus of Van Doren that led to Berryman's decision to become a poet. And in the summer of 1935 Berryman's elegy "Note on E. A. Robinson" appeared in *The Nation*,[31] an auspicious beginning for a poet who was only twenty.

The poet's days at Columbia were not without difficulty. He encountered prejudice against Jews and Negroes, and he was repelled by it.[32] Despite his new gregariousness, he claims to have been able to relax more at the Apollo, a movie and vaudeville theater on 125th Street in Harlem, than in Hartley Hall, the Columbia College dormitory where he and his friends congregated ("Nowhere," *Love & Fame*, 20). At Columbia, his academic career was twice threatened. He explains in *Love & Fame* that his pursuit of a girl from Smith College caused him to lose interest in everything academic, and to fail Van Doren's course in eighteenth-century literature ("Down & Back," 15).

Berryman had written a satisfactory final examination for the course but, in a mood of honesty toward Van Doren and masochism toward himself, he appended a comment that he had read only seventeen of the forty-two books required. Van Doren's remarks on the examination paper were that, despite its quality, he felt compelled to fail Berryman in the course. As a result, Berryman lost a scholarship and was required to drop out of Columbia for a semester, a move that the dean of the college felt would give the young man time to regain control of himself. After a few months of unprodigal reading and private study, Berryman returned with an extensive notebook; Van Doren changed the grade, and the scholarship was restored. Berryman proceeded to make grades high enough to qualify for Phi Beta Kappa and to be awarded a fellowship for additional study.

With the fellowship money Berryman planned to attend Clare College, Cambridge; but during his last semester at Columbia he almost failed to graduate at all. He explains the situation in "Crisis" (*Love & Fame,* 27-29). He was required to take seven courses during his final term, and a grade lower than B in any of them would prevent his graduation. Unfortunately he became involved in a personal conflict with Emery Neff, his professor in a course in nineteenth-century literature. Berryman consciously irritated Neff in every way possible, rudely interrupting him, asking him arch and impertinent questions throughout the semester, and urging his fellow classmates to do the same. Neff was made extremely uncomfortable and retaliated by not having the course grades posted until after he had departed for Europe. Berryman's grade was a C.

Van Doren, the dean, Berryman's adviser, and, according to the poem, all the senior faculty members of the English department were edgy before the mark was posted and embarrassed when it was, for they had participated in electing Berryman to Phi Beta Kappa and in awarding him the Kellett Fellowship, Columbia's finest traveling award. Worried about what Neff might say, but even more disturbed by the prospect of a Phi Beta Kappa who might not graduate, the dean, Van Doren, and the adviser Gutmann chose to administer a second examination. When Berryman did well on it, his course grade was changed to a B. He received the Bachelor of Arts degree from Columbia in the spring of 1936.

After collecting the first installment of his fellowship, Berryman spent the summer in a small town near Montreal ("Recovery," *Love & Fame,* 30). In the fall, he was at Clare College, where his studies went more smoothly than at Columbia; he was appointed the Oldham Shakespeare Scholar for 1937. During his two years abroad he found time to grow a beard; to engage in a serious love affair; to meet William Butler Yeats, W. H. Auden, and Dylan Thomas; and to make trips to France and Germany—events which are of approximately equal importance in later poems. He received the Bachelor of Arts degree from Cambridge in 1938.

III   *Launching a Career*

When Berryman returned to New York, he behaved strangely for a poet ready to begin a career. He "applied for a job as an advertising copywriter. He failed to get it—partly because of the beard and partly because he had had the innocence to suggest that an insurance company adopt as its symbol the Rock of Gibraltar, unaware that a rival concern had already thought of the idea."[33] He remained in New York during the academic year 1938-39, wrote many poems there, and became a friend of Delmore Schwartz,[34] whose first book of poetry and prose had just been published. During the summer of 1939 Berryman vacationed with friends in Grand Marais, on Lake Superior;[35] and, in the fall, he began his teaching career at Wayne University (now Wayne State) in Detroit. He remained there only one year, concurrently serving as poetry editor of *The Nation,*[36] and then accepted a Briggs-Copeland instructorship in English composition at Harvard. He taught at Harvard for three years, from the fall of 1940 through the spring of 1943.

In 1940, Berryman's first collection of verse, "Twenty Poems," was included in *Five Young American Poets.* In 1942, a second collection, *Poems,* was published; and in October of that year, on the eve of his twenty-eighth birthday, he married his first wife, Eileen Mulligan. From 1943 to 1951 Berryman was intermittently a fellow and lecturer in creative writing at Princeton University. He received Rockefeller fellowships in 1944 and 1946, a grant-in-literature from the National Institute of Arts and Letters in 1950, and a Hodder fellowship for 1950-51.

During his stay at Princeton his writing increased in depth, breadth, and recognition. His short story "The Imaginary Jew" won the Kenyon Review-Doubleday award for 1945. The story is a recollection of an event that had occurred in New York in the summer of 1941 when Berryman had been accused of being a Jew by a belligerent young Irishman.[37] The theme is the brotherhood of man, but the story is weakened by the presentation of the Irishman as a stereotype—"a muscular fellow . . . with heavy eyebrows, coatless, plainly Irish."[38] Another short story, "The Lovers," was written about the same time as "The Imaginary Jew"; and it is as clearly autobiographical. The setting is Long Island during Prohibition; the tone is F. Scott Fitzgerald's; the theme is the hopelessness of an obsessive love, both for the young protagonist and for an older family friend who is in love with the boy's mother.[39]

IV *The Crane Study*

While at Princeton, Berryman published more poetry and critical prose than fiction. *The Dispossessed,* his third collection of poetry, was published in 1948;[40] reviewers praised it for its technical control but generally were not enthusiastic. Berryman's major work of scholarship, *Stephen Crane,* a critical biography, was published in 1950;[41] and this book was more a cause of the Crane revival than the result of it, since the last previous biography of Crane had been Thomas Beer's in 1923. Berryman's volume was received with mixed reviews, although there was considerably more praise than blame. Praised for its sensitivity and perceptiveness, it was criticized for a lack of restraint, a strange prose style, and especially for the attempt to understand Crane's life and art by an appeal to Freudian psychology. The reviewers easily found examples to attack.

Berryman's enthusiasm is evinced in such statements as "By a margin [Crane] is probably the greatest American story-writer, he stands as an artist not far below Hawthorne and James, he is one of our few poets, and one of the few manifest geniuses the country has produced."[42] An example of the style: "We are interested not only in what Stephen Crane *did* but in what we find there is evidence that he was compelled toward."[43] And a typical passage of Freudian analysis reads: "Now Maggie is not being rescued *from* the water but *to* it—exactly as we are about to see George's mother being. By some frightening twist, Crane's fantasy had to secure father-identification by drowning the actual mother-representative."[44] Berryman defended himself against the charge of amateur psychologizing by pointing out that the reviewers themselves had little knowledge of Freudian psychology and were hardly capable of judging his use of it (*Stephen Crane,* xi-xii).

A fair judgment of the work seems to be Edwin H. Cady's, who is appreciative of the biographical sections, but doubtful about the psychologizing. He concludes that the volume "stands beside Beer as an indispensable adjunct" to Crane studies.[45] William J. Martz has done Berryman's *Stephen Crane* a disservice by quoting a reviewer's comment about his "inability to reduce his insights to reasoned discourse . . . ,"[46] as if that characterizes the entire book; the reviewer was referring to only one chapter of it. In simple clarity *Stephen Crane* compares favorably with most critical prose.

Berryman's enthusiasm for Stephen Crane was partly a result of several coincidental similarities between the two writers. Each was born of devout parents but took a strongly independent religious position. Each, as a child, was relatively slight in build. Each revered his father and felt abandoned at his father's death (Crane was eight when his father died). Each had suicidal impulses, felt compelled to travel and to write, and had undergone a traumatic experience when he was a preadolescent (Berryman's was to suffer his father's suicide: Crane's, to witness a white girl being stabbed by her Negro lover).[47] Finally, as we shall see in Chapter Four, Berryman found in Crane illustrations of a peculiar kind of irony and of a theory of the origins of poetry that the poet consciously adopted in *The Dream Songs.*

V   Poet, Teacher, Critic

In 1951, the poet left Princeton to pursue his academic career at the University of Cincinnati, where he was Elliston Lecturer in Poetry during 1951-52. He received a Guggenheim Fellowship in 1953, traveled in Europe, and completed the long poem *Homage to Mistress Bradstreet.* In the spring of 1954, he taught in the creative writing program at the State University of Iowa, and he taught at Harvard that summer. In October of 1954, he became an instructor in the humanities program at the University of Minnesota. There he conducted two courses: one in American civilization, the other in comparative religion.[48] He was regarded as something of an absent-minded professor in dress and manner, but as a popular and successful lecturer.[49] He also taught as a visiting professor at several other universities—at Berkeley in 1960, at Indiana in 1961, and at Brown in 1962-1963—but refused even to consider job offers from the South because of its endemic racial prejudice. In 1957, he made a two-month lecture tour of India for the State Department.[50] Granted a second Guggenheim Fellowship and a sabbatical leave in 1966, he spent the school year in Ireland, where he frequented pubs, visited literary and historical landmarks, and completed his *Dream Songs.*[51] In 1967, he was awarded a ten-thousand-dollar grant by the National Endowment for the Arts; and, in 1969, he was named a Regents' Professor by the University of Minnesota, the highest honor available to a faculty member.

Although Berryman's academic career progressed smoothly after 1939, the poet's personal life was always plagued with difficulty. In 1947, he suffered a disastrous love affair—one of "dozens," the poet claimed[52]—that drove him to severe mental disorder. A colleague at the time recalls that no one "drank, danced, talked, or even chased women with the abandon Berryman brought to these activities.[53] The poet underwent psychoanalysis from 1947 to 1953, a therapy which helped him recover from the love affair;[54] but his first marriage ended three years after he and his wife separated in 1953, and "his heavy drinking and the tensions accompanying the writing of *Homage to Mistress Bradstreet* [acted] as causes. . . ."[55]

In 1956, Berryman married his second wife, Ann Levine,[56] to whom the slim volume *His Thought Made Pockets & the Plane Buckt* (1958) is dedicated. A son, Paul, was born in 1957; but this marriage too ended in divorce in 1959.[57] In 1961, the poet married Kathleen Donahue,[58] a girl twenty-five years younger than he.[59] Kathleen legally changed her name to "Kate" in deference to her husband's wishes.[60] A daughter, Martha (named after the poet's mother)—called "Twissy" by her father—was born while the poet was teaching at Brown University in 1962-1963. A second daughter, Sarah Rebecca, was born in June 1971. At the time of Berryman's death the family lived in a frame house on Arthur Avenue in Minneapolis, the first home the poet had owned. Despite his successes — personal, academic, aesthetic — the poet continually suffered from recurring nervous disorders, although his last two books of poetry, *Love & Fame* and *Delusions, etc.,* were calmer in some ways than anything he had written in two decades.

Throughout his career Berryman published, in addition to his poetry, a wide range of criticism and scholarship—on Shakespeare, Thomas Nashe, "Monk" Lewis, F. Scott Fitzgerald, Ezra Pound, and others. During the 1960's, while he was busy writing Dream Songs, his critical output diminished, but his interests continued to be broad. Toward the end of his life, he had several works in preparation: a translation of Sophocles,[61] several works about Shakespeare, a book describing Berryman's travels in America and elsewhere, a volume of transcribed dreams,[62] and a novel, *Recovery*.[63] These works were not completed, for on January 7, 1972, Berryman leapt from a bridge in Minneapolis to a frozen riverbank of the Mississippi; he was killed instantly. He was fifty-seven years old. The possible causes of his suicide are both legion and uncertain: he never overcame the loss of his father; he had a serious drinking problem; his health was failing; he left a note saying that he considered himself a "nuisance" to family and friends; he may have felt that he could never surpass *The Dream Songs*. Whatever the immediate motive, the loss to American letters was an unfortunate one.

CHAPTER 2

The Early Poetry

THE first two collections of Berryman's early work—"Twenty Poems," in *Five Young American Poets* (1940), and *Poems* (1942)—contain verse written in 1940 or earlier. Sixteen of the poems in these collections were reprinted in *The Dispossessed* in 1948, a convenient date to take as the end of the early period. With its useful introductory note unfortunately omitted, *The Dispossessed* was reprinted in the volume *Short Poems* (1957).

The fifty poems of *The Dispossessed* are arranged into five sections. The first of these has, the poet says, a "thematic" order (*The Dispossessed,* vii) but I am unable to discover it. Whatever theme the seven poems in this section share may have been deduced after they were composed, for the first four of them are reprinted from the earlier collections and therefore were written before 1940. The following four sections of *The Dispossessed* are arranged "roughly [in] their order of writing" (*The Dispossessed,* vii). The twenty-four poems of sections II and III are dated 1940 or earlier, with the exception of "Boston Common," which has for its setting and approximate date of composition February 1942. Section IV of the volume contains "Canto Amor" (dated 1944-45 by the phrase "my thirtieth year"), a group of nine poems called "The Nervous Songs," and two poems written around 1947. Section V consists of seven poems written during 1947-48.

I *The Early Poetry: Borrowed Voices*

About one-third of the early poems, especially those written before 1940, were strongly influenced and sometimes dominated by the voices of other poets. In 1965, Berryman pinpointed the sources of this early style; first, he says, he imitated "Yeats, whom I didn't so much wish to resemble as to *be,* and for several fumbling years I wrote in what it's convenient to call 'period style,' the Anglo-American style of the 1930's, with no voice of my own, learning chiefly from middle and later Yeats and from the brilliant young Englishman W. H. Auden. Yeats . . . could not teach me to sound like myself (whatever that was) or tell me what to write about."[1]

The Yeats influence on the early poetry is seen in various devices. The basic trimeter line pattern of "On the London Train"[2] (*Short Poems,* 19-20) and "The Apparition" ("Twenty Poems," 57) may have been learned from Yeats's "Easter 1916" or sections of "The Tower." The refrain, sometimes italicized as Yeats's usually were in his *Last Poems,* occurs in "River Rouge: 1932" (*Poems,* 7), in "Thanksgiving: Detroit" (*Poems,* 16), and most noticeably in "White Feather" (*Short Poems,* 54). The last is a retelling of a humorous and grotesque incident that occurred in Australia when a young lieutenant returns from the war after losing an eye. He is dressed in civilian clothes and is handed a white-feather, a symbol of cowardice, by a female passerby. He pops out his artificial eye and places it in the woman's hand, although he thinks at the time that, for all he or anyone else knows, every man is a coward. The refrain, *"The eye stared at the feather,"* is Yeatsian both in the directness of the image and in its suggestiveness.

Among other influences, a Yeats-like admiration for one's forebears is seen in "Ancestor" (*Short Poems,* 33-34), a poem that honors Berryman's great-grandfather, a Confederate general who fought at Shiloh, repudiated the Klan-ridden South, went into exile in Honduras, and finally returned home as a federal sheriff or marshal in blue uniform. We learn the ancestor's name—"Shaver"—in "A Point of Age" (*Short Poems,* 9) and in Sonnet 76 the poet would again write about him. Yeats's ambivalence toward man's physicality is mirrored in Berryman's two poems entitled "The Animal Trainer" (*Short Poems,* 42-45). Reminiscent of Yeats's "The Circus Animals' Desertion," Berryman's animals represent the sexuality, tension, and excitement that the poet at once despises and requires for the creation of his art. However, Yeats's influence is most pervasive in four meditative lyrics—"Meditation," "At Chinese Checkers," "The Statue," and "A Point of Age." Three of these are divided into numbered stanzas in the Yeats manner, and all are based on the eight-line stanza, with various line lengths and rhymes, of Yeats's "In Memory of Major Robert Gregory" and other poems of his middle period.[3]

"Meditation" ("Twenty Poems," 58-60) is based on the Yeatsian *ottava rima* stanza but adds a line to it. In the poem a young man who must be equated with the poet sits in his Cambridge room on a rainy day and recalls his boyhood at school, his dedication to his craft, and a disquieting love relationship. "At Chinese Checkers" (*Short Poems,* 37-41), written during the summer of 1939, is a clearer poem. In it, the poet plays the game of the title with three children and recalls his innocent childhood—when he played the same game with a friend named "Baynard" and the friend's sister, when he called out at night for his mother, and when he played football and chipped a tooth.[4] He feels now that something has been lost from those days of golden innocence, but he is unable to articulate exactly what it is.

"The Statue" (*Short Poems,* 4-5), written in New York in 1939, is the only one of the four meditations printed in all three of the collections of early poems. The statue, that of the explorer and scientist Alexander von Humboldt, is described by the poet as looking out over the people of the city—lonely clerks, cripples, misfits, sexual deviates, bums who have slept in the park all night, and strolling couples—all of whom are either unaware of the statue or indifferent to it. The poet associates himself with the statue in an awareness of time and death that others do not possess. The grotesques do not notice the sound of water fountains, even though "their happiness runs out like water. . . . / They trust their Spring; they have not seen the statue." The statue seems to symbolize not only a cynical awareness and resignation but also a kind of aristocratic pride that the poet shares. The people themselves resemble animals: the bums are figured as dogs who are turned out at morning; the lovers are seen as caged and anxious creatures.

Until the last stanza, the poem is impersonal and aloof. The poet's condescension to the bums and lovers, as well as his assumption of final wisdom while still in his middle twenties, is irritating. The final stanza concludes more satisfactorily, however, with the poet himself no longer superior to what he has described. He turns from the scene he has observed, notes the traffic lights and the buildings that lie between him and his own "dark apartment," and imagines himself there later in the evening. Spoken of in the third person he is the

>   insignificant dreamer,
>   Defeated occupant, [who] will close his eyes
>   Mercifully on the expensive drama
>   Wherein he wasted so much skill, such faith,
>   And salvaged less than the intolerable statue.
>   (*Short Poems,* 5)

The fourth Yeatsian meditation, "A Point of Age" (*Short Poems,* 8-12), is even wearier in its controlled despair. Written in Detroit in the spring of 1940, it looks backward for advice to Cotton Mather, Daniel Boone, Ethan Allen, and great-grandfather Shaver; but it expresses no hope for the present or the future. The language of the poem is sometimes borrrowed from Yeats: the mind's changing "Images" may be taken from Yeats's "Among School Children"; and the windy storm that destroys great trees and the threatening birds of prey are the same as those in Yeats's symbology, where they foreshadow the downfall of great civilizations or are metaphors for the corruption of the modern age.

In some of the early poems both Yeats and Auden are operating behind the scenes. "Letter to His Brother" (*Short Poems,* 26-27) anti-fascistically refers to the concentration camp at Dachau but concludes more like Yeats's "Prayer for My Daughter" than a political poem: "May love, or its image in work, / Bring you the brazen luck to sleep with dark / And so to get responsible delight." The technique of slant rhyme ("laughed-left") in this poem and throughout Berryman's verse may have been learned from either Yeats or Auden, both masters of it. "Desires of Men and Women,"[5] a second poem of dual influence, first imagines the kind of aristocratic life that Yeats consistently praised—a great house with heirlooms, servants, and large, high-ceilinged rooms; a place of orderliness, peace, and the social amenities; a manor where the inhabitants follow hallowed custom throughout their daily lives. Such people embody and preserve the civil laws and civilization itself. They attend polite social affairs where they converse in French and behave impeccably. The poem has a line break, a familiar Yeats device; and it mentions a "Cinquecento" piece of jewelry, a word that recalls Yeats's "Quattrocento" in "Among School Children."

But the audience of the poem, the addressed "you," those in the present who dream of such a life, are not aristocrats; they are vulgar members of the middle class, and the poet scores them with an Audenesque sardonicism and irony and impersonality. He says that no one,

> my dears, would dream of you
> The half-lit and lascivious apartments
> That are in fact your goal, . . .
> or dream of you the rooms,
> Glaring and inconceivably vulgar,
> Where now you are, where now you wish for life,
> Whence you project your naked fantasies.
> (*Short Poems,* 28)

An earlier and less successful poem of mixed parentage is "The Trial," written in 1937. This fake-ancestral lament bemoans the decline of a conservative society. The first two stanzas echo Yeats's elegies for the past:

> The oxen gone, the house is fallen where
> Our sons stood, and the wine is spilt, and skew
> Among the broken walls the servants are
>
> Except who comes across the scorching field
> Historian. But where the wind is from
> That struck the mansion, great storms having failed,
>
> No man can say.

The third stanza begins to sound like Auden in its mixture of ancient implements and military sewage disposal: "Prosperous generations, scythe in hand, / Mapped the continents, murdered, built latrines" ("Twenty Poems," 65).

An additional Auden touch is noticeable in an occasional brittle wit: a man dying is described as "graduating" from this life ("The Statue," *Short Poems,* 5); a man killed in an auto accident had made a quick turn and suddenly "he became an angel / Fingering an unfamiliar harp . . ." ("The Moon and the Night and the Men," *Short Poems,* 52); and a Botticelli goddess is called "Venus on the half-shell" ("At Chinese Checkers," *Short Poems,* 41). More distracting than this wittiness are Audenesque lines that describe a general malaise in words of almost total abstraction:

> [This] day in history must hang its head
> For the foul letters many women got,
> Appointments missed, men dishevelled and sad
> Before their mirrors trying to be proud.
>   ("The Spinning Heart," *Short Poems,* 17)

What Berryman has called the "Auden climate" surrounds most of
these early sociopolitical poems, though sometimes it is difficult to
measure. Berryman once characterized poems written in that
climate as being "ominous, flat, and social; elliptical and indistinct-
ly allusive; casual in tone and form, frightening in import."[6]

"The Possessed"[7] (*Short Poems,* 22-23) and "The Curse" have all
of these characteristics except "social." The first poem describes the
arrival of night and the ghosts and the horror they bring. The
narrator asks someone (perhaps himself) to feel guilty about his unspecified sins. Some vaguely dangerous attackers are said to be insistently climbing the stairs, and the speaker points out a knife that
could be used to kill both "Heart & guilt" at once. But whether the
weapon is to be used for suicide or for self-defense is not clear.
Auden's "O What Is That Sound" is similar in its vagueness of setting, detail, and motive, and in the nightmarish horror it attempts
to evoke. "The Curse" ("Twenty Poems," 70) presents a man who
stands at twilight beside a broken wall, and a Gothic house stands
in the background. The descending darkness is compared to
ghostlike sins that both threaten man and inspire him to evil acts.
Only children, idiots, and the dead escape the "universal curse,"
that original tendency toward evil; and the children escape it only
so long as they are young. The primary sin is war itself (the poem
was written in 1938-39), but "war" may also be a metaphor for any
kind of evil conflict between men.

Two of Berryman's prewar poems, "Night and the City" and
"Conversation," perfectly fit his definition of the Auden climate.
The first of these continues as vaguely as it begins:

> Two men sat by a stone in what dim place
> Ravelled with flares in darkness they could find,
> Considering death. The older man's face
> Hollowed the hope out in the young man's mind. . . .
>
>   The air,
> Ironic, took their talk of time and cause

> Up to indifferent walls and left it there.
> ("Twenty Poems," 66)

Similarly, "Conversation" (*Short Poems*, 31-32) never specifies its characters or their fears. The poem's basic metaphor is that of life as a voyage. But, in the prewar world, the ship has slipped anchor and is drifting aimlessly through a dense fog. There are discussions—or arguments—among the passengers, but all agree that they do not know where they are going. Food is running low, everyone is so frightened that he cannot sleep, and the darkness and the depths of the sea offer the only possible harbor—a place of death rather than safety. The real weakness of these two poems is their abstraction—we never feel that a specific conversation takes place in "Conversation" or that "two men" are actually present in "Night and the City."

Berryman did write two Audenesque poems that are more successful because they do specify a setting and clarify the causes of fear and despair. "Nineteen Thirty-eight" begins and concludes with the "great planes" that were beginning at the time to "swarm" like "germs" throughout the world. Successive stanzas refer to the assaults upon China by Japan, the takeover of Austria by Germany, the "island Dove" (England) allowing the "Eagle" of Germany to divide Czechoslovakia, the bombing of Spain by the Luftwaffe, and, finally, groups of surviving guerrillas in any or all of these countries who continue to fight for freedom. The last stanza is a powerful assertion that all men share in the guilt of war:

> The winter sky is fatal wings. What voice
> Will spare the aged and the dying year?
> His blood is on all thresholds, bodies found
> Swollen in swollen rivers point their fingers:
> Criminal, to stand as warning.
> ("Twenty Poems," 69)

The "blood" is a misleading symbol: it seems to be like the blood of the Passover lamb, which identified the houses of the Israelites in Egypt; but in Berryman's poem the blood marks the thresholds of the guilty rather than the innocent.

"World-Telegram" similarly achieves its effect of sadness and horror by a calm recitation of specific facts taken from that New York newspaper of May 15, 1939[8]—a "Man with a tail" who is going to appear at the New York World's Fair, an accident, diplomatic conflicts among the world powers, a five-year-old Peruvian girl who has had a baby, machine guns at the coal mines in Kentucky, King George VI nearing Quebec, the imminent marriage of the film star Robert Taylor, and so on. Most of the details are recorded without alteration, and many of the words are directly from the newspaper. Dudley Fitts, in a generally negative review, still found "World-Telegram" to have "an assured grace and a *pietas*. . . ."[9] But the final lines of the poem are less effective than those which preceded them:

> If it were possible to take these things
> Quite seriously, I believe they might . . .
> Immobilize the most resilient will,
> Stop trains, break up the city's food supply,
> And perfectly demoralize the nation.
>
> (*Short Poems*, 30)

The passage is weakened by its use of the Briticisms "quite" and "perfectly" (which seem to be only padding), by the change of tone from factual to superior, and by the belaboring of the pessimism we have already been led to feel in preceding stanzas.

Four early sociopolitical poems are as absolutist as Auden could be in their assumption of truth and rectitude, but we would be unfair to attribute their manner wholly to Auden. Two of them are blatantly pro-labor and anti-capitalist. "River Rouge: 1932" (*Poems*, 7) describes a strike, a lockout, and a demonstration that had taken place on March 7, 1932, at the Ford plant near Detroit. The police opened fire on the workers, killing three of them and wounding fifty. "Thanksgiving: Detroit" (*Poems*, 16) contrasts the workers and their enemies during another strike and lockout, one that occurred after Berryman arrived in the city in 1939. In this poem the laborers ominously stand and wait in the streets while capitalists enjoy themselves elsewhere, "dancing, drinking, singing vainly." The phrase first means that the bourgeois are guilty of vanity; but, when it is twice repeated, it also comes to mean that their revelry is, or soon will be, ineffectual as a means of escape from the restless and sullen proletariat.

"The Dangerous Year," written on March 1, 1939, similarly attacks capitalists—not for opposing labor but for their greed and isolationism. The poem is a dialogue between the poet and a capitalist who speaks in the first-person plural. The capitalist speaks first, saying that he and his cohorts are vaguely troubled by a "Man of Fear" (Hitler, *Time* magazine's Man of the Year for 1938) and are aware of the conflicts throughout the world, in China and elsewhere; but they are certain that "we have the Atlantic to safeguard us: / No plane can reach our shore." An italicized line concludes the speaker's remarks, and the poet responds to them in words of doom:

> Forget the crass hope of a world restored
> To dignity and unearned dividends.
> Admit, admit that now the ancient horde
> Loosed from the labyrinth of your desire
> Is coming as you feared.
>
> (*Poems,* 3)

Unlike Auden and most anticapitalists of the time, and in spite of his sympathy for labor, Berryman did not have a corresponding admiration for Communism. Perhaps because of his youth during the 1930's, he had escaped the typical view of liberal intellectuals that Communism was an effective force against Fascism and Nazism. That view was shattered when the Communists and Nazis signed a ten-year nonaggression pact on August 24, 1939, which permitted Hitler to invade Poland on September 1 and effectively begin World War II. Russia then invaded the Polish Ukraine on September 17, and in October it forced the Baltic states of Estonia, Latvia, and Lithuania to grant military bases there. "Communist" (*Poems,* 15), which refers to these events, sarcastically attacks both the Russian Communists and the now-disillusioned intellectuals who had trusted them. The form of the poem is the ballad, a form that Auden has parodied. "Communist" specifically parodies the anonymous "Lord Randal," a conversation between a mother and her son, a "handsome young man" who has been poisoned by his "true-love." In Berryman's poem, he is an "honest young man" whose mind has been poisoned by Communism.

One reviewer energetically praised *Poems,* the 1942 chapbook in which these four poems appeared, for "stirring up the right kind of protest and slinging a straight arrow at social and political corruption."[10] Necessarily these four self-righteous political poems seem dated, and Berryman chose not to reprint them in *The Dispossessed.*

The Yeats-Auden influence is, then, very strong in much of the early meditative or political verse. An examination of the basic subjects of the early poetry leads us to several poems in which Berryman was better able to harmonize the echoes of Yeats and Auden with his own voice, and sometimes to escape the echoes entirely.

II   The Themes of the Early Poetry

In addition to sociopolitical concerns, most of the other themes that recur in Berryman's later work are evident by 1948: the nature of art, the conflict between faith and doubt; the academic life; friendship and love; dreams and madness; and, overshadowing all of these, a sense of loss — loss of innocence, love, friends, faith, sanity, or identity. Three of the best sociopolitical poems are "1 September 1939," "The Moon and the Night and the Men," and "Boston Common." These are less acerbic in tone and broader in appeal than, say, "The Dangerous Year." Less willing to fix blame for the war, they convey instead a great sadness at its beginnings.

Although the poem shares the Auden climate, "1 September 1939" (*Short Poems,* 47) only superficially resembles Auden's "September 1, 1939."[11] Berryman, in his poem, is the man who sits on the seashore, tears off bits of cellophane, and helplessly ponders the invasion of Poland, the evacuation of children from London, and the Russian-German pact. The Russian "Bear" finds protection under the wings of the German "Eagle," and the other European nations are figured as small, frightened creatures. The lights of civilization seem to be going out as twilight descends; and the man begins to weep, imagining that Europe will itself be "dismembered" by the Luftwaffe in a manner similar to the cellophane that he has torn apart.

"The Moon and the Night and the Men" similarly presents the poet darkly observing "the night of the Belgian surrender" to Germany on May 28, 1940. He is playing chess with a friend but cannot keep his mind on the game. The two quote Paul-Henri Spaak, leader of the Belgian government-in-exile; and they discuss the future, a time when no man will be able to enjoy literature or the other arts, none will be able to determine his fate, none will be able to say what he thinks. The poet then quotes Henry Adams: "History is approaching a speechless end, / . . . [and] Adams was right." One reviewer feels that the idea is, "like the lines, too limp to live";[12] but the weakness in these lines is alleviated by the careful structure of the poem and by an almost incantatory effect of the repetition of "moon" and "cold," as here in the first stanza:

On the night of the Belgian surrender the moon rose
Late, a delayed moon, and a violent moon
For the English or the American beholder;
The French beholder. It was a cold night,
People put on their wraps, the troops were cold. . . .

A cold night.
(Short Poems, 52)

The significance of the next event in the poem, the death of a "stupid well-intentioned" motorist, is not clear until the final stanza in which the King of Belgium is also called "well-intentioned" and apparently stupid. Leopold III had been a "Roadmaker to hell" by proclaiming Belgium's neutrality in 1937, an unsuccessful move designed to avoid occupation by Germany. The poem last returns to the imagery of the first stanza as the war continues, "and the moon in the breast of man is cold." The symbols of moon-cold-death may be borrowed from García Lorca's *Blood Wedding* but are equally effective here.

A third political poem, "Boston Common" (*Short Poems,* 59-64), was written a few weeks after America had entered World War II. A Yeatsian meditation, it achieves a lofty power of its own. The poem is an attempt to define heroism; and it begins by praising Robert Gould Shaw, the Union hero who led the first regiment of Negro troops to fight in the Civil War. Shaw and nearly half his soldiers were killed in their attack in 1863 on Fort Wagner, South Carolina. The poet stands before the Saint-Gaudens monument to Shaw and his men and calls them "Immortal heroes" (stanza II). He is not being ironic in doing so, but he soon insists that the true hero is not a man of war and may even be the common and casual bum who has fallen asleep below Shaw's cenotaph (stanzas I, IV).

This man, the poet says, turns away from the glory of war and derides our worship of war heroes. Instead, he is imagined by the poet to admire men who may be of different religions, philosophies, or nationalities, but who work for peace. Such heroes, whatever their actual occupation, are figured as Candide-like tillers of the soil, taking care of their gardens and working only so that all mankind may enjoy the beauty and goodness of life (stanza XIV). Their work is called "violent," both because of the dedication and energy behind it and because it must at times result in armed conflict, as the examples in stanza XV make clear: Lincoln, Mao Tse-Tung, Teng Fa (an early associate of Mao's), and Tracy Doll (a labor leader imprisoned in Detroit in 1939).[13] The quality of their intention is what distinguishes the violence of these men from that of glory-seekers or aggressors; the poem implies that men like Lincoln and Mao fought wars only with the intent of securing peace—a paradox that "Boston Common" never adequately resolves.

The villain in the poem is aggressive and total war itself. War is compared with sex, a "Congress of adolescents, . . . / Bestial and easy, issueless" (stanza V). War is "issueless" in the sense that it does not resolve the issues and also because, in the metaphor, it has no offspring. War is a "brothel" where, instead of a marriage between the common man and the angel of truth and justice, the only kind of ceremony possible is one in which a "Hobbledehoy" of the air corps mounts his bomber. His moment of climax is his moment of death (stanza VII). The implied comparison of the young pilot aboard his metal bomber to Shaw astride his bronze stallion subtly alters the unalloyed praise for Shaw in stanzas II and III.[14]

The poet argues against the childish desire of some men to become war heroes by saying that, as often as not, officially recognized heroes are no more than "swine" (stanza VIII). He invokes the ghost of William James, the speaker at the dedication of the Shaw memorial in 1897, who repeats that such monuments are often simply "Accidents of history."[15] The ghost of James, which continues to speak to the poet, tells him that true heroes should perhaps have no memorials at all since men tend to forget their war heroes of the past (stanza IX). The poet agrees, imagining the many nameless and dead "defenders of our time, / From Spain and China, . . . / Leningrad, . . . Corregidor . . ." (stanza X). He has only respect for these men who were willing to die in defense of their homes, men who fought back with their knees or fingernails or any weapons at hand (stanza XI). He concludes that we might honor heroic action if we must, as he has honored Shaw; but his final command is for us and the common man, even the sleeping bum, to become "kicking" and "working" men (stanza XVI), like those in stanza XI who used their knees to defend themselves, or like those in stanza XV who labored for the common good.

"Boston Common," like the earlier meditations, may be too directly reminiscent of Yeats to project a "clearly identifiable voice,"[16] but its sensitive thought and its compassion are telling. Those readers who agree with Dudley Fitts that the "Yeatsian ancestry" of the poem is "unintegrated"[17] may prefer "The Pacifist's Song" (*Short Poems*, 76), written only two or three years later and entirely unlike Yeats. The poet, or his *persona*, is more explicitly pacifistic here than in "Boston Common," saying that killing in war is murder, even a form of fratricide because all men are born of the Earth Mother. He insists that he is like other men in most ways, but cannot deny that he is pulled by some kind of life-force away from the murder of war; and, even though he is not guilty of such murder, he is visited in his nightmares by the horrid dead, their eyes empty and sad. When he awakens, he hears someone—or his conscience—telling him that he must not kill, that he must accept any suffering without resorting to violence. The poet concludes that he must ignore the patriotic insistence of his countrymen that he fight and kill, for he has international sympathies; he rejects chauvinism and mourns the deaths of all men. The attitudes in this and the other sociopolitical poems persist throughout Berryman's later work: the sympathy for the underdog—for labor around 1940—tends to shift toward Jews and blacks; but the liberal, antitotalitarian, pacifistic stance remains the same.

The nature of art is one of the themes of "Winter Landscape," the best of the early poems. A detailed description of Pieter Brueghel's sixteenth-century painting *Hunters in the Snow*, the poem is in blank verse and all in one slow sentence. It presents three hunters, carrying spears and accompanied by their hunting dogs. The group is returning to its village at dusk, and the men seem to be exhausted as they trudge through the snow, passing other townsfolk busy at play or at various tasks. Although the poem includes many minute details from the painting, it concentrates on the three hunters, men who

> Are not aware that in the sandy time
> To come, the evil waste of history
> Outstretched, they will be seen upon the brow
> Of that same hill: when all their company
> Will have been irrecoverably lost,
>
> These men, this particular three in brown
> Witnessed by birds will keep the scene and say

By their configuration with the trees,
The small bridge, the red houses and the fire,
What place, what time, what morning occasion

Sent them into the wood, a pack of hounds
At heel and the tall poles upon their shoulders,
Thence to return as now we see them and
Ankle-deep in snow down the winter hill
Descend, while three birds watch and the fourth flies.
                                        (*Short Poems,* 3)

Berryman felt that this was his first poem which did not sound like "Yeats or Auden—or Rilke or Lorca or Corbière or any of my other passions of those remote days."[18] Several critics have praised the poem, and Robert Lowell has called it his "favorite Berryman poem" of the early period because of its "gentleness and delicacy and clarity."[19] Despite the apparent simplicity of "Winter Landscape," it poses several difficulties. Berryman once complained that the poem is usually taken "for either a verbal *equivalent* to the picture or (like Auden's fine Brueghel poem, 'Musee des Beaux Arts,' written later) an *interpretation* of it. Both views I would call wrong...."[20]

The poet directs us to an article by Arthur and Catherine Evans that posits the first view. These two aestheticians feel that the poet's intent is "to rival the peculiarly painterly exposition of an idea through a parallel reconstruction by means of verse."[21] Berryman agrees with several affinities discovered in the article and quotes from it: "... They say the poem's 'elaborat[ive] sequence urged on by the sweeping carry-over lines' (they mean run-on)—within the stanza or between stanzas—preserves the same order of presentation and the same groupings of elements as the Brueghel composition. . . . Purposefully restricting himself to a diction as sober, direct, and matter-of-fact as the painter's treatment of scene and objects, Berryman so composes with it that he achieves an insistent and animated pattern of strong poetic effect.' "

But, Berryman, comments, "Nowhere is anything said as to what the poem is *about*...." He then explains that the poem "dates from 1938-9 and was written in New York following two years' residence in England, during recurrent crises, with extended visits to France and Germany, especially one of the Nazi strongholds, Heidelberg. So far as I can make out, it is a war-poem, of an unusual negative kind. The common title of the picture is 'Hunters in the Snow' and of course the poet knows this. But he pretends not to, and calls their spears (twice) 'poles,' the governing resultant emotion being a certain stubborn incredulity—as the hunters are loosed while the peaceful nations plunge again into war."[22] These are wild and whirling words indeed. Berryman claims to have discovered, in writing "Winter Landscape," that "a poem's force may be pivoted on a missing or misrepresented element in an agreed-on or imposed design. . . ."[23] But, without his comments, no reader of the poem could discover the missing element of war or his feelings about it. What Berryman seems to be saying is that the poem means, for him, something other than what it means to anyone else.

Even with the poet's comments, the poem does not seem to be a war poem of any kind. One critic claims that "Winter Landscape" fails entirely to "realize a meaningful theme. . . ."[24] Robert Lowell is closer to the truth in concluding that the poem reproduces the meaning of the penultimate stanza of Keats's "Ode on a Grecian Urn,"[25] the stanza that imagines the "little town . . . emptied of its folk, . . . silent." What Lowell has in mind is our sadness and desolation in the remembrance of things past, and "Winter Landscape" does convey that. But it also suggests another theme of Keats's poem—art is long, life is short. As Berryman's poem states this thought, although all men die, "These men, this particular three in brown . . . will keep the scene . . . as now we see them. . . ." These men live, permanently, because they exist in an imperishable work of art.

Berryman's interest in pictorial art is one element in the "Song of the Man Forsaken and Obsessed" (*Short Poems,* 75). The artist who speaks is Paul Gaugin, the nineteenth-century Frenchman who gave up a business career and a family to live obscurely and to paint vividly in the Marquesas Islands. The theme of the poem is the obsession of the artist with his work and the necessary loneliness it brings.

The theme of the conflict between faith and doubt is seen most clearly in "The Disciple" (*Short Poems,* 6-7). Although the poet felt that Yeats saved him from the influence of T. S. Eliot,[26] this poem necessarily reminds us of Eliot's "Journey of the Magi."[27] "The Disciple" is a monologue spoken by an old man who recalls certain events in the life of Christ, events that he had witnessed years before. The poem tells us of Christ's raising of Lazarus, His com-

passion for the poor and the afflicted, His betrayal by Judas, and
finally His crucifixion. It concludes with a stanza praising a faith
that needs no reason to bolster it:

> I can tell you I saw then
> A terrible darkness on the face of men,
> [Christ's] last astonishment; and now that I'm
> Old I behold it as a young man yet.
> None of us now knows what it means,
> But to this day our loves and disciplines
> Worry themselves there. We do not forget.
>
> (*Short Poems,* 7)

The poem is, then, a hymn on the part of the *persona,* but it is not
simply that. What is most notable about the speaker is his innocence. In the opening stanza of the poem, he remembers being
deeply impressed by Christ's ability to make coins apparently dis-
appear and to draw a piece of paper through a fire without its burning; but he finds the raising of Lazarus to be no more — or
less—impressive than these tricks of legerdemain. Also, the speaker
never mentions Christ's divinity, as if that were unimportant beside
Christ's humane acts. And there are other difficulties. Ian Hamilton
feels that such confusions reveal an ambivalence on the part of
Berryman that makes it impossible to find the poem's "centre";
Hamilton wonders "whether Berryman isn't really floundering
here."[28]

What bothers Hamilton is that Berryman seems to assent to the
old man's faith in the final stanza; but, in the stanza immediately
preceding it, he seems to ridicule such a faith by the use of a series
of puns—"harboured" in the sense of "protecting from the law,"
"coppers" as policemen, "lifted" meaning stolen. Some of the puns
Hamilton objects to do not occur in an earlier version of "The
Disciple" (in "Twenty Poems," 63-64); but their use in either version ought not necessarily lead us to conclude that Berryman is
ridiculing the old man or his faith, or that he is, as Hamilton says,
playing a "joke" on Christ or the policemen or himself.

The old man, in his naiveté, seems not to be aware of the puns.
The poet's use of them, as well as our awareness of them, is a result
of a greater sophistication on his part and ours. "The Disciple"
becomes an ambitious attempt to present the pure faith of an elderly disciple and also to show an awareness of the doubt that of

necessity arises in the modern world. The poet's attitude is ambivalent, expressing both faith and doubt; but there is no ridicule in it. The poem reminds us how simple faith is for the innocent, how difficult for others.

The subjects of the academic life, friendship, and love appear notably in three early poems. "A Professor's Song" (*Short Poems*, 71), one of the "Nervous Songs," satirizes both the professor and the students in his literature class. The professor, who is most concerned about completing an historical survey of Alexander Pope, William Blake, Samuel Taylor Coleridge, and William Wordsworth, quotes a catch-phrase from "Kubla Khan" (" 'That deep romantic chasm' ") and misquotes the "Preface to the *Lyrical Ballads*" (" 'A poet is a man speaking to men' "). He is irritated by his inattentive, sleepy-eyed students; and, when the bell rings, he dismisses them sardonically: "Until I meet you, then, in Upper Hell / Convulsed, foaming immortal blood: farewell." He is slyly accusing his students of the sins of incontinence that are punished in the Upper Hell of Dante's *Inferno*, but he is again inaccurate in having blood there.

"A Poem for Bhain" (*Short Poems*, 58), in tercets, was written for a friend who later, in 1940, died of cancer.[29] The poem, as simple and direct as "Winter Landscape," is a forerunner of the many later poems written for or about the poet's friends. Perhaps less successful is "Canto Amor," a "love song" dedicated to the poet's wife at the time the poem was written (*The Dispossessed*, vii). The poem is not at all direct and is not quite convincing in its joy. It concludes,

> Dance for this music, Mistress to music dear,
> more, that storm worries the disordered wood
> grieving the midnight of my thirtieth year
>
> and only the trial of our music should
> still this irresolute air, only your voice
> spelling the tempest may compel our good:
>
> Sigh then beyond my song: whirl & rejoice!
> (*Short Poems*, 67)

For some reason the poet seems less credible in poems praising his beloved than he is when dealing with the separation of lovers, as in

"Parting as Descent," a poem of 1938 or so. The poet is to catch a train at Waterloo but first spends a few minutes with his friend. When he must leave her, his departure is a journey to hell:

> The bitter coffee in a small café
> Gave us our conversation. When the train
> Began to move, I saw you turn away
> and vanish, and the vessels in my brain
>
> Burst, the train roared, the other travellers
> In flames leapt, burning on the tilted air
> Che si cruccia, I heard the devils curse
> And shriek with joy in that place beyond prayer.
> (*Short Poems,* 24)

The flames and the devils are from Dante; "Che si cruccia" ("he who torments himself") is from Canto XIX, line 31, of the *Inferno.*

The poet's fascination with dreams is seen as early as the vaguely nightmarish "The Possessed" (*Short Poems,* 22-23) and in the coolly clinical "Desire Is a World by Night" (*Short Poems,* 48-49), both written before 1940. One early poem, "The Traveller" (*Short Poems,* 13), seems to be a transcription of a dream. Usually these nightmarish poems imagine death, are populated by horses and devils, and express feelings of sin and guilt—as in "Whether There Is Sorrow in the Demons" (*Short Poems,* 82-83), a title that seems to be borrowed from Scholastic philosophy. This poem also suggests the theme that dominates Berryman's early work and remains important in *Berryman's Sonnets, Homage to Mistress Bradstreet, The Dream Songs,* and *Love & Fame*—the theme of loss.

"The Ball Poem" (*Short Poems,* 14) notes that learning about loss is, like the loss of innocence, a necessary part of maturation. The poet observes a boy playing with a ball that bounces out of his hands, down the street, and into the harbor. The poet says that, with the loss, the boy "senses first responsibility / In a world of possessions," and is being forced to learn the "epistemology of loss." The poet silently sympathizes with the boy, revealing that he too has encountered loss, in a Whitmanesque conclusion: "I am everywhere, / I suffer and move ... / With all that move me, under the water / Or whistling, I am not a little boy." One phrase of the poem, "Balls will be lost always," may support Ian Hamilton's contention that Berryman's poems sometimes have disconcerting private jokes embedded in them; Berryman is elsewhere concerned with fears of castration, and the pun seems inescapable in "The Ball Poem." Whether or not the pun was intended, the poem suffers.

The archetypal loss for Berryman was his father's suicide in 1926, and two of the early poems, "World's Fair" and "Fare Well," have that loss in their background. The first of these has the poet waiting beside a roller coaster for a girl to arrive. He has waited an hour, and his sudden recognition that she is not going to meet him reminds him of another kind of betrayal. He confuses autobiographical and literary memories. First, he is tormented by

> The inexhaustible ability of a man
> Loved once, long lost, still to prevent my peace. . . .
> Childhood speaks to me in an austere face.
> The Chast Mayd only to the thriving Swan
> Looks back and back with lecherous intent, . . .
> Middleton's grave in a forgotten place.
>
> (*Short Poems,* 35)

The allusion is to Thomas Middleton's play *A Chast Mayd in Cheap-side* (1630) and the Swan Theater where it was performed.[30] The reference combines, in a complicated way, love lost with the loss of Berryman's father. In Middleton's play, Tim, a young Cambridge student, writes a letter to his parents, expressing his great love for both of them. In Berryman's poem, the memory of his father obsesses the poet but the grave, like Middleton's, is in "a forgotten place" because the poet had never returned to see it.[31] The "Chast Mayd" who looks longingly after a "thriving Swan" is Berryman's metaphor for the girl he awaits. She, like the unchaste maid in the play who tricks Tim into marriage, is interested only in a "thriving," successful young man. As the poet expected, his friend does not arrive; and he trudges off toward his apartment and his poetry and his "instructor"—the man who first instructed him in loss. "Fare Well" (*Short Poems,* 15) expresses a sense of loss more desperately; the poet despairs of ever remembering his father without undergoing a paroxysm of love and burning resentment. In this poem the phoenix becomes a symbol of the recurring grief. The poet tries to escape from the phoenix's pyre into a restful "snowbed"; the implication is that he will never escape his grief until he himself dies.

Besides the death of his father, the poet had another source for some of the early poems of loss. In 1947, he had the illicit love affair that drove him to severe mental disorder and eventually destroyed his first marriage. At the time, he considered "killing both himself and his mistress because she flatly refused to leave her husband and to marry him."[32] Section V of *The Disposessed* and one poem in section IV, "Surviving Love" (*Short Poems,* 77), seem to have been written during this difficult time. The poet's feelings of madness and his sympathy for a friend who is undergoing similar psychological difficulties is revealed in "A Winter-Piece to a Friend Away" (*Short Poems,* 87-88). His father's death and his own impulse toward death inform "The Long Home" (*Short Poems,* 84-86).

The poet's feelings of loss—loss of stability, identity, and love—expand in the concluding and title poem of *The Disposessed.* The sense of dispossession in it not only is personal but also extends to a view of the world itself in 1947. "The Dispossessed" (*Short Poems,* 94-95) is not, as the poet has claimed, "thoroughly mysterious"[33] but is indeed complex. The setting of the poem is an "empty" house where the poet is reading Luigi Pirandello's play *Six Characters in Search of an Author.* As he reads one line in the play (" 'and something that . . that is theirs—no longer ours' "), he comes to an awareness that "old things," familiar and evil patterns of existence, continually recur. Simply stated, the patterns are political and personal—war and adultery.

The political implications of "The Dispossessed" were first pointed out by John Frederick Nims who, noting the references to German and Italian and recalling that both "Fuehrer" and "Duce" mean "Leader," suggested that the "flying arms" of the second stanza are airplanes and that the "umbrella" of the ninth stanza is a metonym for Neville Chamberlain.[34] The poet also mentions "Stalin," apparently comparing him to Hitler and Mussolini; and he compares all three of these villains to himself and to us, the readers of the poem: their weapons are also "*our* arms," and their story is "our story." No longer is the world a simple melodrama in which evil is easily recognized and overcome ("no hero rides"), for we are all guilty of involvement in war. As the poet explained in an essay in 1949,

everybody is "guilty" of everything, and that is that. . . . Few men of reflection can be satisfied now with their actions and attitudes during the recent war. Well, we put that aside: the Enemy was clear, and moreover what happened (producing what is happening now) would have happened anyway, "It was done for us"—your modern intellectual is astonishingly fatalistic. This is the view generally taken, with a gain in uneasiness, of the use of the atomic bomb. But few men of reflection can be satisfied with their actions and attitudes *now*. Well, again the Enemy is clear (Stalin for Hitler), what is happening cannot be influenced by us, and so on.[35]

The poem also refers obliquely to the atomic bomb—the "weaponeer" arms it, the "cam" of a gunlike mechanism triggers it, and the "umbrella" cloud follows its explosion. (Combining cause and effect, the umbrella could also be Einstein's, mentioned in Dream Song 336.) One result of the bomb's presence is that "Rarely a child sings now," a phrase that occurs in an earlier poem that tells of the death of a culture, "The Song of the Young Hawaiian" (*Short Poems*, 70).

The phrase "cam slid" in the eighth stanza of "The Dispossessed" is a connection between the political and the personal elements behind the poem, for the words occur in Sonnet 70 as a sexual metaphor. Similarly, "the faceless fellow waving from her crotch" in "The Dispossessed" is the poet himself, who in Sonnet 98 climbed up into a sycamore near his lover's house and there also compared her limbs with those of the tree. (The image is from Mallarmé's "Salut": "*De sirènes mainte à l'envers.*") The poet is "faceless" because he has lost his identity by engaging in the illicit love affair, just as the Father in *Six Characters* felt he was losing his when he spoke the line that opens Berryman's poem.

Two additional phrases reinforce the notion that "The Dispossessed" has the love affair behind it. The "Movement of stone within a woman's heart, / abrupt & dominant" may refer either to his lover's leaving him or to his wife's discovery of the affair. The phrase "the spidery business of love" is echoed in Sonnet 88, where the poet's lover is figured as a spider who takes him for a victim. Speaking to women, the poet once said that in adultery, "You behave like a spider."[36] In "The Dispossessed," the poet was observing the dark world situation and finding analogies between it and his own condition.

The themes of Berryman's early poetry remain fairly constant throughout his career; but he always tended to experiment in style. As we examine the style of the early poems, we shall determine which elements of it remain with the poet in his subsequent works.

III   *The Early Poetry: The Search for a Style*

Berryman's career was a "long, often back-breaking, search for an inclusive style. . . ."[37] By 1948, he had written in three fairly distinct styles: one is based on the Yeats-Auden influence, as in "The Statue" or "Boston Common"; the others are best illustrated by the first poem and the last of *The Dispossessed.* The 1939-40 poem "Winter Landscape" is impersonally quiet, relaxed, and graceful. It is consistent in tone and diction, orthodox in its blank verse, relatively clear in meaning. The 1947-48 poem "The Disposesed" is strikingly different. It is more personal, although veiled in its references to the poet's life; it is elliptical, strained, and excited; it mixes levels of diction, wrenches syntax, and is complex and allusive. The style of "The Disposessed" is similar to that of the contemporaneous *Sonnets* and, with them, is a forerunner of *Homage to Mistress Bradstreet* and of *The Dream Songs.*

We must not, however, oversimplify the poet's stylistic development by suggesting that between 1938 and 1948 it underwent an orderly progression. The Yeats-Auden influence was still in force even after the style of "Winter Landscape" had been developed; "Boston Common" was written about two years after that poem. And we can catch undigested bits of Auden's "September 1, 1939" as late as 1947 or so in "Rock-Study with Wanderer" (*Short Poems,* 79). "New Year's Eve" (*Short Poems,* 89-91) is Yeatsian in stanza form and Audenesque in its sardonic tone, although it was written about the same time (1947-1948) as "The Dispossessed." The 1938 poem "Cloud and Flame"[38] (*Short Poems,* 25) is as densely allusive and elliptical as "The Dispossessed." "The Lightning" (*Short Poems,* 78), a poem of 1947 or so, is as clear as "Winter Landscape."

The concurrency of various styles in the early period suggests that Berryman had not found any one style that would be expressive of himself. Indeed, we do not get a clear picture of the poet from the early poems. Sometimes he seems cool and aloof; at other times, passionate and sympathetic; but in either case, he seems to be unwilling to speak about himself except obliquely. Although he disagreed with Eliot's view that poetry should be impersonal,[39] he was unable in the early poems to form a distinct poetic personality. He had not yet learned, as Yeats was forced to learn, that the subject of his poetry at its best was to be 'himself-as-himself' or as an "expressive personality."[40]

Berryman did find two devices in the early verse that would aid him later in overcoming his reticence about self. One, learned from Yeats or Pound, is the *persona,* as in "The Disciple" or "The Nervous Songs," poems in which the speaker sometimes is and sometimes is not the poet himself. The second was the discovery in "The Ball Poem" that, as Berryman said in 1965, "a commitment of identity can be 'reserved,' so to speak, with an ambiguous pronoun. The poet himself is both left out and put in; the boy does and does not become him, and we are confronted with a process which is at once a process of life and a process of art. A pronoun may seem a small matter, but she matters, he matters, it matters, they matter. Without this invention . . . I could not have written either of the two long poems that constitute the bulk of my work so far."[41] The two long poems were *Homage to Mistress Bradstreet* and *77 Dream Songs.* The poet did not mention the *Sonnets,* still unpublished at the time he made these remarks in 1965. In the very personal *Sonnets,* the poet was able to overcome his natural reticence because, at the time he wrote them, he did not envision that they could ever be published.

Only one stylistic quality remains constant throughout the early poetry—the poet's craftsmanship. Sometimes, but not often, it seems to be merely a "delight in craftsmanship" ("Twenty Poems," 47) for its own sake, as in the "Letter to His Brother" (*Short Poems,* 26-27), a poem in which a rhyme pattern (*abbacddc*) is counterpoised against a metrical pattern (5,4,5,5,5,4,5,5). Of course the early poems are not without an occasional weakness. William J. Martz has rightly attacked these lines for their triteness: "The summer cloud in summer blue / Capricious from the wind will run" ("Cloud and Flame," *Short Poems,* 25).[42] He might also have noted the padding and the inversion in the second line, needed to achieve meter and a following rhyme. But to conclude, as Martz does, that Berryman's poetry generally is "sloppy in craft"[43] is absurd. Throughout his career Berryman was considered a "poet's poet,"[44] an epithet reserved for writers of superb technical control.

CHAPTER 3

Poet in Transition

B ERRYMAN'S *Sonnets* (1967) and *Homage to Mistress Bradstreet* (1953) were both begun about the same time that poems in the fifth section of *The Dispossessed* were being written. The one hundred and fifteen *Sonnets,* or most of them, were written during 1947 in a remarkable burst of energy. Only one of them (25) was printed before 1967, in the 1952 anniversary issue of *Poetry* magazine. *Homage* was begun in 1948, but the poet found himself unable to write more than a few lines of it for almost five years.[1]

Both the *Sonnets* and *Homage* have the complex allusiveness and the syntactical twists of "The Dispossessed," but they are more clearly precursors of the Dream Songs in being long poems. In a sense, the poet had solved the problem of style in *The Dispossessed;* but two additional problems remained: one was the problem of personality and how to express it; the other, form. Berryman solved the first in the *Sonnets,* in which a distinct poetic personality emerges. But in form the *Sonnets* were a dead end; a poet cannot continue writing only sonnets if he expects to be taken seriously in our time. *Homage* solved the problem of form with an inventive stanzaic pattern, but it relapsed into veiled reticence about the poet himself. The problems were not be be resolved concurrently until the poet began writing Dream Songs, although the *Sonnets* and *Homage* do have excellences of their own.

Apparently the poet did not feel that, in writing the *Sonnets* or *Homage,* he had solved either the problem of finding an expressive personality or a suitable form, for he wrote several short poems in the 1950's that are very much like the early poetry. These were published in *His Thought Made Pockets & the Plane Buckt* (1958), first printed in a limited edition and then reprinted in *Short Poems* in 1967.

I *The Players of the* Sonnets

The *Sonnets* describe a violent and destructive love affair between a university poet-in-residence and a Danish-American beauty called "Lise." Both the lovers are married—the poet to "Esther"(83), Lise to an unnamed man who is somewhat older than she and who may be a colleague of the poet's (42). Esther is also a beautiful blond, but she sharply contrasts to Lise in her mild humility, her dependence upon her husband, and her devotion to him. She is described as having been lonely all her life until, the poet condescendingly remarks, he befriended her (69). Lise's cuckolded husband is said by the poet to be a "friend" (52), a man of goodness and kindness (21) who can be at times serious, at times informal and relaxed (42). Although the poet once fears that Lise's husband suspects the lovers (21), that good man seems to remain forever unaware of his wife's indiscretion (33). The two couples become friends soon after the affair begins and seem to remain so throughout its development (30, 33, 109, 110). Lise's marriage is unaffected by her activities, but the poet's wife begins to suspect her husband's infidelity early in the affair (33), soon confirms it (69), and their marriage is, or soon will be, destroyed. Esther and Lise's husband remain shadowy figures since the *Sonnets* belong to the lovers; about them we learn a great deal.

Lise's blond hair and gray eyes are mentioned repeatedly, and she is also described physically as being "breasty" (14) and as having a "small mouth" (1) and a "switching walk" (39). Like her lover, she was born in Oklahoma under the sign of Scorpio (appropriately, since the genitals are associated with that astrological sign). She had an unhappy childhood (18). Her father was in the oil business in Tulsa (80). Lise is, at the time of the affair, about twenty-seven (91) and has a young son named Peter (95). She lives with her husband in a "stone home" (10, 52) that has a "sycamore" tree in the yard (10, 98) and that is not far from the poet's house.

Other details about Lise and her surroundings are more revealing of her personality. She usually dresses informally in shorts and a blouse (22, 77) or in "blue jeans & a sweater" (115). She consumes prodigious amounts of beer, scotch, and rum (24, 30, 37). She can feel contrition for burning dinner (18, 19) but not for her adultery. When she is not out of town or on their hillside with her lover, she spends much of her time lying barefooted on the floor of her home, drinking and listening to classical music (37, 92). Despite her love of music, she is indifferent to these lyrical sonnets written for her and to her (92).

Usually gay and flip, Lise can occasionally lose her temper over some trifle, and once she breaks a knuckle as she smashes some household items (18). Generally, she seems to exist in a state of childlike mindlessness (" 'Why do you love *me?*' " she asks the poet, in Sonnet 24), but she can be forward, even physically aggressive, in the exercise of her athletic lust (4, 67). She is unwilling to divorce her husband (76), probably because that would be inconvenient. Finally, she is careless in her manipulation of the poet, reminiscent of Scott Fitzgerald's Daisy Buchanan in *The Great Gatsby*. At one point, Lise swears that she will never leave her lover (34); but, before long, she is casual in announcing her faltering devotion, writing him a note that says only, " *'I am not the same'* " (94).

The protagonist of these *Sonnets* is a widely read, sensitive man who, until he meets Lise, is dedicated to his work. He is more complex than she is. He can be a proud man, egotistically contemptuous of his associates (53). He is obviously pleased with himself for having met Yeats, Dylan Thomas, and Eliot (5) and for owing three letters to Ezra Pound (27). He insists at the height of the affair that Lise will always remember him (49), and he recounts his heroic feats of sexual prowess (74). But he can also be humble and self-effacing when he contrasts his verse to that of Andrew Marvell or François Villon (32); and, Keats-like, he says at one time that his poetry will not live (40). The poet shares Lise's propensity for lust but can also feel guilty about it (35, 45, 46). He can be incautious and afraid (1, 33), joyous (67) and sad (35, 64), impatient (60) and long-suffering (98). He can be both humorously scatalogical (85) and moralistic (45). In short, he is a man presented in all his complexity.

The unhappy outcome of the affair is a result of the conflicting personalities and motives of the two lovers. The poet tries at one time to claim a reckless abandon similar to Lise's. First he recites an incident of her youth when, as a seventeen-year-old girl, she and a boyfriend (who later became a criminal, the poem says) got drunk and rode their horses out one dark night in full knowledge that a storm was gathering. When it broke, the two whipped their mounts, repeatedly galloping them near the edge of a dangerous crevasse (91). In a companion sonnet he implicitly compares her wildness to his when, as a child, he fearlessly climbed an oil derrick and began the move to his present impetuous recklessness (93); but he concludes this poem with a wish for calm and propriety rather than for excitment and danger. He hopes that someday he will be able to live respectably with Lise, to have dinner with her, and to accompany her to bed without guilt or fear of discovery.

The poet's love for Lise causes all sorts of conflicts in him because he does not have her amoral strength. He feels guilty about neglecting his wife (69) and his work (103), about his hypocrisy and lies (83). He takes ethical principles seriously, realizing from the first that his adultery is opposed to the religious "Law" he frequently mentions. At first, he is torn between the law of love and the religious law, and he wishes he could observe one or the other rather than being trapped between them (34). Once, he recalls his youthful respect for the religious law and claims he did not realize that his love for Lise would deny that law. He remembers reading, as a twenty-one-year-old man, one of John Donne's sermons or meditations in which adultery is described as a crime usually perpetrated at dusk. He disagrees with the time since he and Lise usually meet at dawn, and he recalls his youthful and intolerant disgust at even the possibility of adultery, insisting that no one could even consider stooping to desecrate the marriage vows.

But he realizes that now he has become the very thing he once despised, lawless and irresponsible, lost in a series of lies to his wife and in debilitating fears that his duplicity will be discovered (45). Soon afterward, he capitulates to Lise and says that he is willing to live by the law of love alone (55) as it becomes his "Faith" (67, 99) and Lise becomes his "goddess" (90). But he cannot deny the religious law for very long; he realizes that the only way to salvage anything from the relationship is to unite the two laws by marrying Lise (19, 69, 93). She is equally determined that the affair remain one only of the flesh (76).

II *The Setting of the* Sonnets

The locale of the *Sonnets* is never specified, but is clearly Princeton, New Jersey. The alumni who return for a bicentennial celebration (20) wear blazers of orange and black, Princeton's colors (17). Sonnet 26 recalls the township during the Revolutionary War and then describes the present nonindustrial com-

munity of academics and men of substance, a place where manufac-
turing plants are not permitted for fear, the poet says, that the
"professors" and the "millionaires" and their Negro servants might
be disturbed. A "tiger" out of British heraldry is then described as
having migrated to the New World; and it now rests there, comfortable, domesticated, well-fed, and "substantially dead"; the tiger is
of course, the totem of Princeton College. Other indicators of the
locale are more veiled: the buildings called "McIntosh" (106) and
"Upper Wyne" (53) are probably McCosh and Lower Pyne, actual
halls at Princeton. "Knowlton Street" (20) may be the Charlton
Street on the campus.

The publishers are understandably vague about the time of the
affair ("during the 1940's," a blurb says) but that also is clear.
Berryman speaks of himself as being thirty-two (105), his age during most of 1947. And he mentions an incident that occurred, just
before the affair began, on a Thursday "In Nineteen XXXX,
February / Twice-ten-day" (106). The only Thursday, February
20th, that fell during Berryman's tenure at Princeton was in 1947;
and "forty-seven" is the only year of that decade that fits the meter,
with a syllable for each of the X's. The reference to Princeton's
bicentennial celebration also coincides with 1947.

Three of the *Sonnets* do, however, suggest a later date. One of
these refers to a "sonic boom" (112). Since the first supersonic
flight did not occur until October 14, 1947, and then in California,
it is unlikely that Berryman heard it. But he may be speaking
metaphorically, not having heard a sonic boom but hearing about
it. The second possibly anachronistic reference is to Anne Frank,
the victim of Nazism (113), whose diary was first published in
Amsterdam in June 1947, but was not published here until 1952. It
is unlikely that the poet read the book during the summer or fall of
1947, even if he did somehow see a copy of it, since he obviously was
busy with other matters. A third sonnet describes the gulled lover as
being an "ass" for three years (105), but a chronology of the
Sonnets reveals that the affair could not have lasted three years: it
started in the spring and ended the following fall. Perhaps the poet
was an "ass" in carrying the burden of his teaching and writing
duties for three years, but in these poems he is Lise's lover for only a
few months. The conclusion is not that 1947 is an inexact date for
the affair but that Berryman must have written or rewritten a few of
the *Sonnets* at a later time. William Meredith has noted that the last

four poems, "like the Dream Songs, have initial capitalization only where it coincides with prose capitalization," indicating that they were probably added at a later date.[2]

The specificity of the setting, time and place, makes it clear that the *Sonnets* not only "seem to be autobiographical"[3] but are. The poet refers to himself once by his last name (84); and, although "Esther" and "Lise" are pseudonyms (as the poet has indicated[4]), they were actual people. That does not mean that the poet has failed to embody his experience in art, and it does not mean that anyone should begin to seek out the actual identity of "Lise." It does mean that the *Sonnets* are more than a literary exercise. They are intensely felt embodiments of personal experience and form a part of the imaginative autobiography that the poet was to continue in the Dream Songs.

III   *The* Sonnets: *Chronology and Development*

The *Sonnets* are only generally in chronological order since most of them are recollections, but the sequence of events is fairly clear. Sonnet 106 recalls a time before the affair began, a stormy February evening the poet first saw Lise—or, if the brazen, strange young lady in the poem is not that lovely blond, she is at least some Eve-like creature who tempts the poet. Unlike the original Eve, Lise does not offer her victim the apple itself, for she has already eaten it, metaphorically, down to the "core." She then plants the sinful seed in the poet's previously steady and responsible heart.

Like Sonnet 106, Sonnet 1 must have been written after the affair was over; but it recalls a time about a month after that first temptation in February. The poet is figured as a traveler in a desert who encounters a mirage-like poisonous well, a well which might give him nourishment except that he notices the bones of a dead creature nearby. His emotions were, in March, a mixture of desire and fear. He longed for Lise to allow him to enter her life but, he adds,

> who not flanks the wells of uncanny light
> Sudden in bright sand towering? A bone sunned white.
> Considering travellers bypass these and parch.

The second stanza of Sonnet 1 illustrates, incidentally, that the poems are not in the order in which they were written; it describes the poet's feelings after the conclusion of the affair:

> This came to less yes than an ice cream cone
> Let stand. . . .
>   Luck lies with the bone,
> Who rushed (and rests) to meet your small mouth, risk
> Your teeth irregular and passionate.

The 'ice cream cone" suggests the transcience of the affair and also tells us that the poet himself, or a fellatious part of him, is the "bone" that "rushed (and rests) to meet" Lise's mouth. The image of fellatio may not be explicit here, but its recurrence elsewhere makes it clear (3, 6, 7, 59, and Dream Song 183). The implication is that Lise will cause, or has caused, the poet's death. Whether his death lies in the past, the present, or the future is intentionally obscured by the use of both past and present tenses in line thirteen, "rushed" and "rests." The device of mixed tenses allows the poet to present his feelings as the events were occurring and also in retrospect; his love and his later awareness of the destructiveness of it are simultaneously presented. This double view is one of the real achievements of the sequence for, as readers, we are aware of both views throughout the *Sonnets* while the lover is, in a sense, only partly aware of them. Such a point of view also gives the *Sonnets* a sense of inevitability similar to that of tragic drama. We are made aware from the first of the certain outcome of the affair.

The poems are arranged, then, neither strictly in the order of the events nor in the order in which they were composed. Like Sonnet 1, the second Sonnet was written after the events it describes. It quotes a desperate vow that the poet had made a "month" before, probably sometime during April, that, whenever he next saw Lise, he would simply pass her by. Sonnet 42 recalls the next stage of the affair, quoting a comment made by Lise as she confronted him: " 'I *want* to take you for my lover' "; his April promise now forgotten, the poet answers, "*Do.*" The affair was consummated on May 3, and the pair "writhed" for a "month," "in sudden love like a scrimmage" (70). But it is likely that sometime during May, Lise is away briefly, visiting somewhere west of New Jersey. Even the towers of Princeton are said to notice her absence (9). In Sonnet 13, the poet himself has made a brief journey to another state, also probably during May.

The lovers are separated throughout June and the first two weeks of July (70). The poet and Esther are vacationing in Connecticut part of that time, probably throughout June. The poet is at a loss without his love. Unable to sleep, he wakes up early and tries to think of ways to occupy his time. He recalls his farewell to Lise after their twenty-four days together during May, and he regrets the wasted month of June. It has been unpleasant, boring, and hot—a time of unfulfilled passion for him (41). While in Connecticut, the poet and his wife abstractly discuss divorce (56). Neither of them mentions the affair specifically, but Esther by this time has begun to suspect it (33), and the poet has begun to consider marriage with Lise (19, 56).

When Esther and the poet return to Princeton, perhaps around the first of July, Lise and her husband are away and someone is staying temporarily in their house (43, 52, 54). Sonnet 50 mentions that the poet has been writing these love poems for "two months," probably May and June. The poet seems not to have returned in time to see Lise leave, since in Sonnet 49 he mentions a good-bye note, a daisy, and a photograph that she had left for him in their grove. But Sonnet 27 suggests that the poet may have seen her briefly before she left; he says he has missed her for about two weeks. In either case, she has departed by July 3 and seems to have gone to the beach; the poet keeps looking for her car to return, and all cars he sees resemble "Beachwagons" (62). Lise is still absent in Sonnets 54, 55, and 59. Sonnet 60 anticipates her return, and by Sonnet 64 she is back but has not yet arranged to see her lover. Her failure to do so may be simply that she does not want to make her husband suspicious, but earlier she has been brazen in her management of the affair, even arranging to kiss her lover while his wife and her husband are in the house with them (33). More likely she is beginning to tire of the affair, as is suggested in Sonnet 68, where the poet vainly waits for her as it begins to rain. She has told him that if it rains she will not be there; but again, earlier in the affair, rain did not seem to dampen her enthusiasm. Sometime before July 18 (74), Lise has returned and meets the poet on their hillside (67). Either late in July or early in August the poet goes to a farm near "Kingston," Pennsylvania to visit a friend named "William" (78). His wife is quite likely not with him, for he seems to be alone as he rides a bus back to Princeton (82). Also, while in Pennsylvania, he had received a postcard from Lise which suggests that her passion has not cooled (80), a note she would not likely have written if Esther were with her husband. Although there is no explicit indication that Lise is not contented with her lover at this time, their conflict is beginning to form even before the poet's trip to Kingston. The poet expresses his dissatisfaction with their illicit relationship and his desire to possess Lise entirely:

> I bare the quick of the have
> And have not, half have, less than half, O this
> Fantasy of your gates ajar, gates barred.
> Poaching and rack-rent do you hope will save
> True to ourselves *us,* darling?
>
> (76)

Sometime in August, Lise may be away again (84), but this poem may be one describing her absence in July. In August, after the poet's return from Kingston, the lovers meet and the poet's continued insistence on marriage causes Lise to become distinctly cooler. He realizes that the affair has been, for Lise, only an idyllic and temporary arrangement, and he generalizes about all women, saying that they do not want to hear anything from their lovers that threatens to disrupt their lives. Her coolness causes the despairing poet to hope no longer for marriage; he wishes only that the two of them remain, for a while, in love and in bed (90). A few days later Lise writes her note saying *" 'I am not the same' "* (94). Two references to "August" (102, 110) and a phrase referring to the "four months" of the affair (103) indicate the time. After a few poems of sadness, as the poet realizes the affair is over, he becomes bitter and sardonic. Speaking of himself in the third person, he says that "he was had", and, in a wry sea-shanty line, he says that he should have stayed with his wife (107). In its lack of initial capitalization, this poem is like Sonnets 112-115; therefore, it was probably not written in 1947.

Another poem of bitterness indicates the time as late September or early October. Lise is ironically described not as a "sister-in-law" but a "sister-outlaw" who is and has been "laid" for a month in some distant place. The poet then angrily lists his obligations to Lise. He sardonically thanks her for long evenings when he was at her house (apparently with others present also, perhaps at a party) and yet was unable to get her alone. He thanks her for the two letters she has written to him—only two, while he had written more than a hundred poems to her. And he thanks her for the infrequent times when he almost succeeded in stopping her incessant chattering (108).

In Sonnet 110, Lise makes it clear that the poet will not be welcome to visit her alone but, in her blitheness, sees no reason why the two couples cannot remain social friends. The poet, who figures himself as a victim of Nazism, becomes "Moses" while Lise becomes a member of the *Schutzstaffel,* Hitler's elite corps of special police. Since she is called a "strip-murderer," she may also be Ilse Koch, the wife of the commander of the concentration camp at Buchenwald; Ilse reportedly owned lamp shades made out of human skin. Lise carries a "whip" and a fingernail file, the one a torture instrument, the other an indicator of her insouciance. The poet salutes Lise's proposed duplicity with a Nazi "heil." The date given for this poem, August 27, conflicts with the time indicated in Sonnet 108 (at least "four weeks" after Lise's note). Again, Sonnet 110 may be one of the many poems in the sequence which are not in chronological order.

One phrase in Sonnet 110, "hoping *I* endure," suggests the effects of the affair on the poet. Not only has his marriage to Esther been destroyed, but his very identity has also been threatened. Earlier in the affair he had seen it as a means of fulfilling both himself and Lise: "To become ourselves we are these wayward things" (45). But, by Sonnet 88, he has begun to doubt his identity; he compares himself to Don Quixote, who also claimed to know who he was while lost in illusion. And, after Lise's letter, his identity is gone; his *"name"* and his self have become dissociated (96).

The last Sonnet signals approaching fall. In the chill of pre-dawn, the poet climbs to the lovers' trysting place, carrying his Sonnets to read to Lise if she by some chance is there. As he half-expected, she is not; and she does not arrive: "Presently the sun / yellowed the pines & my lady came not / in blue jeans & a sweater. I sat down & wrote" (115). The poet's hopeless love will continue, we assume, for a long time, sometimes in daydreams (114), sometimes in nightmares (79, 104), but it will be as futile as regret.

IV   *The* Sonnets: *Tradition and the Individual Talent*

The poet of these sonnets writes within two intertwining traditions of his genre: that of romantic love and that of the sonnet form. The conventions of romantic love, or Courtly Love, were first

developed toward the end of the eleventh century in the poetry of
the French troubadours. According to the conventions, a married
lady was to be venerated, placed on a pedestal, where she inspired a
lover to great and glorious deeds. Her lover, her knight in shining
armor, was to fall madly in love with her, to be immediately taken
by her bewitching charms. Sometimes a glance was enough to capture the lover; at other times, a love potion was helpful or
necessary. The drinking of such a potion indicates the qualities of
uniqueness and inevitability in romantic love; the lovers are fated
for each other alone, as if their love were determined by the gods or
destiny. The beloved and her knight were then to engage in illicit
love with the tacit approval of the husband, but only after the
knight had courted his lady with religious devotion and suffered
great torment and despair.

Such adultery obviously was inimical to Christian ethical concepts, but the churchmen adopted some of the other conventions of
romantic love. The glorification of the aristocratic lady and her inspiration of her thrall became, in Catholicism, veneration for the
Virgin Mary. Hence also, we have the inspiration of Dante's beloved and untouched Beatrice as that fourteenth-century poet
journeyed through hell and toward heaven in his *Divine Comedy.*
All suggestions of adultery and of lust are dropped. Another resolu-
tion of the conflict between Courtly Love and Christian morality
was the attachment of the conventions to unmarried lovers who
find fulfillment only in marriage.

In some Medieval romances, the conventions of Courtly Love are
in conflict with traditional morality. In the twelfth-century tale
Tristan and Iseult, for example, the lovers observe most of the conventions. Inadvertently, they drink a love potion and are thereby
fated to fornication and later adultery; Iseult is described vaguely
and conventionally as being beautiful and blond. But the husband
of Iseult, King Mark, is unaware of the deception practiced on him
and is unhappy when he learns about it. The lovers themselves must
die because of their sinful behavior, although in some of the various
versions of this romance they are buried side by side, and rose
bushes intertwine above their graves.

The association of illicit love with death in *Tristan and Iseult*
became one of the conventions of romantic love in a Christian
culture. We may also note the frequent separations and difficulties
the lovers face as they pursue their passion. According to Denis de

Rougement in his *Love in the Western World,* such separations were even sought by the lovers as a stimulus to passion. He feels too that the association of passion with death is itself a kind of death-wish. In this tradition of romantic love modified by Christianity, Francesca Petrarca, or Petrarch (1304-1374), wrote his sonnets to "Laura," the real but unattainable woman of his inspiration.

Petrarch popularized the sonnet form, which had been invented not long before him, and created many of the conceits that influenced sonneteers throughout Europe. In England, Thomas Wyatt (1503?-1542) translated some of Petrarch's sonnets from the Italian and the next few decades saw many poets adopt Petrarch's metaphorical conventions: "A lady's eyes were suns; her hair, gold wires; her lips, coral; her cheeks, roses or cherries. A lover's heart was a storm-tossed ship; love, the star he steered by . . . ; his tears were rain, his sighs gales."[5] Love is a flame, or a fiery thirst. Chivalric metaphors—knights, ladies, warfare—are frequent. Teeth are pearls, hearts break with unrequited or unfulfilled love, the lover suffers feverishly.

Other English poets of the sixteenth and seventeenth centuries—Philip Sidney, Edmund Spenser, Christopher Marlowe, Shakespeare, Robert Herrick, Andrew Marvell—used these metaphors in their love poetry; but of these poets who wrote sonnets few followed the difficult rhyme pattern of Petrarch. The Petrarchan or Italian sonnet allows only two rhymes in the first eight lines, called the "octave" or "octet," for the pattern is *abbaabba.* The concluding six lines (the "sestet") have only two or at most three rhymes. The pattern here varies; the sestet can rhyme *cdecde, cdcdcd, cedced,* or in almost any other combination except that it tends not to conclude with a couplet (only four of Petrarch's do so). Such a rhyme pattern is more difficult to achieve in English than in Italian because of the relative paucity of rhyming words in our language. This difficulty was avoided in the so-called "English" or Shakespearean sonnet, which retained Petrarch's fourteen pentameter lines but rhymed *abab, cdcd, efef, gg.* In thought, the English sonnet tends to fall into two or three parts with a summarizing couplet that often sounds repetitious or too pat. Petrarch's stanzaic pattern normally suggests a break, a "turn," between the octave and the sestet. In the octave, a thought or metaphor is presented; and, in the sestet, that idea or comparison is expanded or contradicted or altered in some way to bring the poem to a satisfactory conclusion.

The long traditions of romantic love and of the sonnet form set up resonances that strengthen Berryman's *Sonnets*. The poet's complete familiarity with the traditions allows him to follow them, modify them, or parody them in ways that are his own. The notion in romantic love that the lovers are unique is repeated here (86), despite frequent comparisons of these two with lovers of the past—with Tristan and Iseult (109), Petrarch and Laura (15), Odysseus and Circe (4), Glaucus and Scylla (77), David and Bathsheba (21), Oedipus and Jocasta (96), Aeneas and Dido (55), Dante and Beatrice (38), Astrophel and Stella (16), Balzac and Hanska (28), Stephen Crane and Helen Trent (99), and others. The inevitability of their love is claimed in Sonnet 70, as the huge hand of God or Destiny turns a vise that compresses the two of them. Similarly, in Sonnet 106, the cogs of time or the universe itself catch the poet; the "meshing of great wheels" fails to warn him of their inexorable turning.

Love and madness are occasionally equated (65, 79); love and death frequently are. Sometimes, his death alone is implied (1, 7, 12, 19, 31, 73); at other times, both lovers are to be subject to death (38, 57). The two "die" simultaneously in Sonnet 71, repeating the sexual pun that often occurs in Donne and other seventeenth-century poets. Conventionally, the love of these *Sonnets* is a "storm" (50, 82) or a "Fire" (6,7). Images of medieval warfare (46, 16, 97), of flowers (39), and of the Petrarchan ship recur. In Sonnet 25 the poet is the mad captain of a vessel that veers from its course as the poet turns farther away from his wife. Sonnet 15 is itself a translation of Petrarch's Sonnet clxxxix. The octave reads:

> What was Ashore, then? . . Cargoed with Forget,
> My ship runs down a midnight winter storm
> Between whirlpool and rock, and my white love's form
> Gleams at the wheel, her hair streams. When we met
> Seaward, Thought frank & guilty to each oar set
> Hands careless of port as of the waters' harm.
> Endless a wet wind wears my sail, dark swarm
> Endless of sighs and veering hopes, love's fret.

Berryman's translation is better than Sir Thomas Wyatt's and also more accurate. Wyatt renders Petrarch's "Scilla and Caribdi" as "Rock and Rock"; Berryman translates it "whirlpool and rock."

Lise is in many ways the conventional beloved. She bewitches the poet as Circe tried to bewitch Odysseus; he becomes her "swine-enchanted lover" (4). He drinks her "witch-antinomy" (33) as Tristan drank the love potion. She is figured as a "Lady" (1) who inspires her lover to write his poems (92), but who also tortures and torments him (6). Like Laura or Beatrice, Lise is frequently associated with light. Her "eyes light" (13) and she herself becomes light in many poems. In Sonnet 1, she is a well "of uncanny light." In Sonnet 2 the brilliance of her "cloud-gold" hair survives her absence: "Your shining—where?—rays my wide room with gold. . . ." She "blaze[s]" (49); she is "sun incomparable" (77); she is "sunlight" itself (27), appropriately enough, since the rain that falls frequently threatens to darken the "dawn" of the assignations (11, 15, 68). She shines more brightly than "Venus" (66). Even toward the end of the affair, when she has lost some of her brilliance (90), the poet pleads with Lise to "Dazzle, before I abandon you, my eyes . . ." (112).

In most of these comparisons Lise is the idealized and stereotyped lady of love poetry; but the power of the *Sonnets* derives more from the way Berryman individualizes his beloved. Lise is once figured not as a graceful sailing vessel but as a wrecked oil tanker—appropriately, since she drinks so much and since her father was an oil businessman. Her teeth are not perfect pearls; they are "irregular" (1). Her aggressiveness, her lust, her shallowness, her informal manner of dress, her speech show how fully she differs from ideal ladies she is so often compared with. If she inspires the poet to art, she also inspires him to feats of sexual activity (74). She may be light itself, but she is also compared to "gin-&-limes"(43). She may bewitch the poet, but more often it seems that she is simply tricking him by means of the old shell game (14). Her overwhelming power is compared to that of a subway train (60). Finally, the torment to which she subjects her lover is hardly genteel; she is like an Inquisition or Kafkaesque "rackman" (6), a prankster who shoves a billiard ball into her lover's mouth (14), or a "cleaver" ready to slaughter her sheep (62).

Other conventions are similarly altered. Like Shakespeare's sonnet 130, Berryman's 103 parodies the clichés of traditional love poetry ("broken heart," "torment," "storm"). If the lovers are like the great ones of the past, they are also like a team of draft animals (55, 58). The all-consuming fire that threatens to burn down the poet's dwelling does not do so; instead, the house falls over as Lise leans on it, in a bitterly comic comparison of the poet with a helpless little man: "A stronger house than looked—*you leaned,* and crash, / My walls and ceilings were to be walked on. — / The same thing happened once in Chaplin, how / He solved it now I lose" (101). The poet's madness is sometimes less a lover's moonstruck lunacy than a clinical neurosis (79). Finally, their love does not conclude in death, as it did for Tristan and Iseult; at the end of the affair, the poet has "not expired / but [is only] half-dead with exhaustion, like Mr Bloom" (112) of James Joyce's *Ulysses.*

The highly original language of the *Sonnets* resembles that of *The Dream Songs* more than that of traditional poetry. The poet delights in using words differently: "slow" (5), "talon" (44), "throes" (23), and "piston" (60) become verbs; "castaway" (64) becomes an adjective; "grovel" (42), a noun. The level of diction can descend from the wittily formal (policemen are called "azure minions of our law" [54]) to the colloquial ("Plumped for a rose" [3]) to the downright vulgar and scatalogical (109). The poet is able in one poem to mix "Diminutive" and "alkahest" with "poontang" and "horny" (104). Only occasionally does the diction entirely fail, as in the Hollywood Western lingo of "to walk tall" (114) or in the silly pun of "a ton of Styx" (46).

Just as Berryman modifies the themes, the metaphors, the tone, and the language of love poetry, so does he also experiment with the techniques of the sonnet form. The metrical and rhyme patterns of the *Sonnets* are most often those of Petrarch, but metrical and stanzaic variations occur occasionally, as in the added line of 4, 5, 49 and others. More noticeable are the pyrotechnics of rhyme, as in Sonnet 11, where assonance approximates rhyme, or in Sonnet 30, where the poet rhymes "tea" with "wholly," mixing masculine and feminine endings. Sometimes rhyme is achieved by hyphenating words (97, 18), a device learned, perhaps, from E. E. Cummings.

These experiments are a means of working within the very difficult rhyme restrictions of the Petrarchan form. The usual devices for achieving the rhymes in a Petrarchan sonnet are to pad the line or to invert the normal syntax, both of which are technically weak. Berryman prefers ellipses to padding, and he seldom inverts phrases to achieve rhyme. One noticeable and unhappy exception occurs in Sonnet 20 "Two centuries here have been abused our youth." But such forcing is easily forgiven when we notice that the poem limits itself to four rhymes throughout. Curiously, Berryman inverts many phrases within the line—"a kiss blind" (33), "one step false" (33), "Grossly however bound" (34). The purpose is not to achieve rhyme but to give the *Sonnets* an effect of archaism. Frequently the poet complicates his task by adding internal rhymes, out of what must be a delight in craft (111).

The technical brilliance of the *Sonnets* may in itself be what led some critics to remark that the poems lack depth of emotion.[6] This charge is the standard one made against the restrained academic poetry of the 1940's and 1950's; and, though it applies reasonably well to some of Berryman's early verse, it does not to the *Sonnets*. Their technical control forms a contrast to the fragmentation of the poet's self, his loss of identity, his sense of guilt and dispossession; but the depth of feeling seems to me undeniable. An example is Sonnet 73, in which the poet recalls Franz Kafka's short story "In the Penal Colony" (1914) and asks someone—or anyone, but especially Lise—to explain what the story means. His question is only rhetorical, for he realizes his own guilt and the certainty of punishment:

> I am the officer flat on my own machine, . . .
> On whom the mort-prongs hover to inscribe
> 'I FELL IN LOVE'. . . .
> Now the harrow trembles
> Down, a strap snaps, I wave—out of control—
> To you to change the legend has not budged
> These years: make the machine grave on me (stumbles
> Someone to latch the strap) 'I MET MY SOUL.'

In Kafka's story such an infernal machine slowly inscribes the crime of the offender on his body by means of a needlelike device called a "harrow." When he finally realizes what his crime is, the machine kills him by driving a spike through his skull. Like the officer in the story, Berryman operates the machine and also ends up on it himself, although in the poem the death-needles of the harrow, rather than a single spike, kill him, implying a slow death rather than the instantaneous one granted the officer. The poet says that he "met his soul" by engaging in the affair, but he does not mean that he found fulfillment in it; rather, he discovered that he could trespass against the moral law in ways heretofore detestable to him.

He has learned more about himself, but the knowledge is devastating.

The theme of the *Sonnets* is this sense of loss—loss of love and of identity. In theme and in technical accomplishment, the *Sonnets* are not inherently different from other Berryman poems written before 1948; but they do represent a step beyond "Winter Landscape" or "The Dispossessed" in their presentation of deep, personal emotion. In this quality, and in their being a series of related poems (perhaps really one long poem), the *Sonnets* foreshadow *The Dream Songs*.

Berryman's not publishing the *Sonnets* when they were written suggests that he was a poet of two voices, one public and one private. The public voice could write a restrained, impersonal, academic poem such as "New Year's Eve" about the same time the private voice was writing the frank and impassioned *Sonnets*. The public and the private voice could not merge into one poetic personality for several reasons. In the late 1940's, frankness about one's deepest emotions or frankness of language and scene was simply taboo in poetry. Since the 1940's, however, a movement toward personal poetry—"confessional" poetry as it is now called by several critics—has made revelations of the most private emotions more acceptable. Also, during the 1950's, the Beat poets—Allen Ginsberg and others—popularized the tendency toward frankness of language that Ezra Pound and then E. E. Cummings had practiced. By the middle 1960's any word might be found in the poetry of the little magazines, any scene might be described, and any emotion expressed.

In a sense, the passing of time is what allowed the two voices of Berryman to merge; but by the middle 1950's, as he began to write Dream Songs, he was continuing to develop the device that would make it possible for him to express a poetic personality—the device of the *persona* of Henry and others in *The Dream Songs*. Before he made this device his own, his poetry took a self-effacing turn in *Homage to Mistress Bradstreet*. Although Anne Bradstreet is in some ways a mask for Berryman, she reveals very little about him.

V Homage to Mistress Bradstreet: *Subject, Structure, Theme, and Style*

The apparent subject of *Homage to Mistress Bradstreet*, Anne

Bradstreet (*ca.* 1612-1672) is remembered as the first poet in America rather than for the quality of her verse. She was born in England, a daughter of the Puritan Thomas Dudley, secretary to the Earl of Lincoln. She married Simon Bradstreet in 1628 and in 1630 journeyed with him and her father to Massachusetts aboard the *Arbella,* a ship named after a lady who also made the voyage. Mistress Bradstreet suffered through the hot summers and intense winters of the New World, bore four sons and four daughters, and wrote poetry soon after her arrival and throughout her life. In 1647 John Woodbridge, a pastor, returned to England with her poems and had them published there in 1650 under the title *The Tenth Muse Lately Sprung Up in America.* Among others are poems called "Quarternions"—"The Four Elements," "The Four Humours," etc. The large influence on this work was Guillaume du Bartas (as translated by Joshua Sylvester), but there are touches of Francis Quarles, John Donne, and others. Following her death in 1672, a second edition of this work was published in Boston (1678) and included the "Contemplations," a poem of thirty-two stanzas that is usually considered her best work. Anne Bradstreet's father was a public official (he died in 1653) who was involved in the banishment of Anne Hutchinson. Mistress Bradstreet's husband, who outlived her twenty-five years, served as governor of the Massachusetts colony.

Homage is in part a recounting of Anne Bradstreet's life, incorporating fact and phraseology from her writings, Helen Campbell's biography of her (1891), the Winthrop papers, and other sources (*Homage,* 30). But Berryman has consciously altered several factual details of the poetess's life. He has Thomas Dudley, whom he calls her "fierce dogmatic old father[,] . . . die blaspheming, in delirium."[7] He makes Anne the "closest friend" of Anne Hutchinson (30); a reviewer says that there is "no evidence" for such a friendship.[8] He has Ann Bradstreet left severely marked by smallpox, although the poetess claims to have been fully "restored" by God.[9]

One reviewer feels that *Homage* attempts to be a biography of Anne Bradstreet and is therefore weakened by such alterations.[10] Robert Lowell is more accurate in calling *Homage* "the most resourceful historical poem in our literature."[11] "Resourceful" suggests a dependence on sources and also an imaginative recreation of them so that the work can, like George Bernard Shaw's *Saint Joan,* comment on our time as well as the past.

The choice of Anne Bradstreet and her time as subject for
Homage was partly the result of Berryman's interest in America's
past, as in "Boston Common." Berryman felt a connection to the
American past through his forebears: " . . . All my people have been
here since the Revolution—that's a long time."[12] Why he chose
Anne Bradstreet specifically is a more difficult question since he
once suggested that he cared neither for her nor for her work and
called her "this boring high-minded Puritan woman who may have
been our first American poet but is not a good one."[13] But a later
remark is more accurate: "I don't like her work, but I loved her—I
sort of fell in love with her. . . ."[14]

One thing that must have attracted Berryman to Anne was her
forceful and intelligent personality, as it is expressed in the fifth
stanza of "The Prologue" to the "Quarternions":

> I am obnoxious to each carping tongue
> Who says my hand a needle better fits,
> A Poets pen all scorn I should thus wrong,
> For such despite they cast on Female wits:
> If what I do prove well, it won't advance,
> They'l say it's stoln, or else it was by chance.[15]

These are strong words to be expressed in a culture in which women
were considered inferior and where such peccadilloes as smiling or
whispering in church could result in the offender being placed in the
stocks (*Homage*, stanza 16). Perhaps too Berryman admired the
Puritan streak of ethical uprightness in Anne Bradstreet. Some of
his early poems (for example, "Desires of Men and Women") are as
intolerant of man's sexuality as Puritanism could be; and
Berryman's admiration for Anne's purity occurs in *Homage* even as
he tries to woo her—saying that he longs for her—and insists at the
same time that both he and she are "quick to no tryst" (stanza 25).
Most importantly, Berryman admired her for overcoming "the
almost insuperable difficulty of writing high verse at all in a land
that cared and cares so little for it."[16] Ironically, in Anne
Bradstreet's time a woman was considered a domestic creature and
insufficiently bright to compose verse; Berryman once complained
that in our time poetry is considered "effeminate."[17] Both poets
therefore had to face a culture that accused them of taking inappropriate masculine or feminine roles. Like his enthusiasm for

Stephen Crane, Berryman's attraction to Anne Bradstreet was, then, a result of several shared qualities and circumstances.

The theme of *Homage* is bound up in the five-part structure of the poem. An explanation has been given us by the poet:

An American historian somewhere observes that all colonial settlements are intensely conservative, *except* in the initial break-off point (whether religious, political, legal or whatever). Trying to do justice to both parts of this obvious truth—which I came upon only after the poem was finished—I concentrated upon the second, and the poem laid itself out in a series of rebellions. I had her rebel first against the new environment and above all against her barrenness (which in fact lasted for years), then against her marriage (which in fact seems to have been brilliantly happy), and finally against her continuing life of illness, loss, and age. These are the three large sections of the poem; they are preceded and followed by an exordium and coda, of four stanzas each, spoken by the ' I ' of the twentieth century poet, which modulates into her voice, who speaks most of the poem. Such is the plan. Each rebellion, of course, is succeeded by submission, though even in the moment of the poem's supreme triumph—the presentment . . . of the birth of her first child—rebellion survives.[18]

This simplification of structure and theme does not account for much overlapping throughout *Homage* of the sources of Anne's discontent, her characteristic emotion. For example, her "rebellion" against her marriage is present not only in the third section of the poem (stanzas 25-39) but also earlier, as in stanza 15, where she is bored with her husband: "Drydust in God's eye the aquavivid skin / of Simon snoring lit with fountaining dawn / when my eyes unlid, sad." At various places in the poem she is bored with her domestic chores of cooking, washing, and caring for children (stanzas 11, 16, 40). Her discontentment with domesticity is what drives her to her love duet with the modern poet, a surrealistic scene of unconsummated love between what Berryman calls a "witch-seductress and demon-lover."[19] And her rebellion against her environment occurs not only in the second section (stanzas 5-25) but also later, as she sadly recalls the many colonists who have died (stanza 44).

Nor does the poet's summary of theme suggest Anne's rebellion against elements of Puritanism. Sometimes she is bored with its simple piousness that is as tiresome and depressing as a steady rain (stanza 15), or with the colorless Puritan clothes (stanza 22). She is deeply disturbed by the intolerance shown Anne Hutchinson (stanzas 24-25), by the Puritan tendency to quibble about details of faith

and doctrine ("Our chopping scores my ears" [stanza 22]), by the
harsh punishments dealt out to supposed offenders (stanza 16), and
by the simple answers given to difficult questions about death and
immortality (stanzas 23, 41).

Always, as the poet has said, Anne's discontent ends in submission. The reason she submits is that she has a great desire to be
good and assumes that her discontent is sinful. Throughout the
poem, she assumes that her illnesses (smallpox, rheumatic fever,
dropsy) are God's punishment for her sinful feelings. After every
slight rebellion, she experiences great remorse and feelings of
worthlessness before a mighty God, insisting that she is "unfit" for
heaven (stanza 53). In the end, the poet tries to reassure her of her
worth and offers her a "candle," his poem, in homage:

> —You are not ready? You áre ready. Pass,
> as shadow gathers shadow in the welling night.
> Fireflies of childhood torch
> you down. We commit our sister down.
> One candle mourn by, which a lover gave. . . .
>
> (stanza 54)

Anne seems to realize what no critics have noticed about
Homage—that the modern poet and his age are as important to the
poem as Anne Bradstreet and the Massachusetts colony. "Sing a
concord of our thought" (stanza 32), she tells him; and, as he sings,
he reveals that he too is subject to an hostile environment and that
modern Americans feel as betrayed as Anne did by the dream of the
New World. All Americans are called "Strangers & pilgrims" who
have journeyed in search of a "City"—the Just City or the City of
God (stanza 8). The modern poet experiences artistic exile just as he
imagines Anne to have suffered it: "Both of our worlds unhanded
us" (stanza 2). The poet shares Anne's discontent with theological
quibbling but is more openly dissident than she is. She could retreat
into a belief that "God awaits us" (stanza 34), but the poet is doubtful and associates his doubt with a sense of his own fragmentation:

> —I cannot feel myself God waits. He flies
> nearer a kindly world; or he is flown.
> One Saturday's rescue
> won't show. Man is entirely alone

> may be. I am a man of griefs & fits
> trying to be my friend.
>
> (stanza 35)

The poet tells us in a note (*Homage*, 31) that the "Saturday's rescue" refers to the *deus ex machina* of the movie serials he watched as a child. It is the same melodramatic rescue that he longed for in "The Enemies of the Angels" (*Short Poems*, 56) and "The Dispossessed" (*Short Poems*, 95), but which will not arrive in a modern world. In *Homage*, again as in "The Dispossessed," he refers to war ("foxholes") and the atomic bomb ("reactor piles") as symbols of the lostness of our time (stanza 55). *Homage* is not simply "about the woman," as Berryman has claimed (*Homage*, 30); its subject is the poet and America, both early and late.

Certain other emotions in *Homage*, emotions that Berryman shared with his created lover, suggest a deep personal element in the poem. Anne's discontent with domestic life, her desire for a true lover, and the conflicting desire to obey the law of uprightness are emotions expressed by Berryman in the *Sonnets*. Specifically, two passages in *Homage* make the connection. First, Anne Bradstreet speaks one of Lise's lines: "I *want* to take you for my lover." And the poet responds as he did in the *Sonnets:* "Do" (stanza 32). Second, Anne is troubled by the same ethical concerns as the poet in the *Sonnets;* she foresees in her relationship with him "annihilations of law / which Time and he [God] and man abhor . . ." (stanza 28).

As he did in the *Sonnets*, the poet here expresses the desire to obey the religious and ethical law ("refrain / my western lust" (stanza 33]), but is again unable to control his passion. He is driven to the same despair, guilt, and self-denigration that Anne experienced. He is convinced that he is evil: "I trundle the bodies, on the iron bars, / over that fire backward & forth; they burn; / bits fall. I wonder if / *I* killed them. Women serve my turn" (stanza 34). Just as he had comforted Anne, trying to convince her of her inherent worth, so also she comforts him, telling him as Jocasta told Oedipus that his supposed sins occur only in sleep: "—Dreams! You are good." The poet, who cannot share her certainty, insists he is worthless (stanza 34). The sense of personal dispossession and despair is I think the dominant emotion of the poem, but the failure to meaningfully articulate that emotion, finally the failure to express the personality of the poet himself, weakens *Homage*.

In several ways the style of *Homage* is, again, similar to that of the *Sonnets* and "The Dispossessed." An example is this climactic and orgasmic passage in which Anne gives birth to Samuel, her first child:

Women do endure

I can *can* no longer
and it passes the wretched trap whelming and I am me

drencht & powerful, I did it with my body!
One proud tug greens Heaven. Marvellous,
unforbidding Majesty.
Swell, imperious bells. I fly.
Mountainous, woman not breaks and will bend:
sways God nearby: anguish comes to an end.
Blossomed Sarah, and I
blossom. Is that thing alive? I hear a famisht howl.

(stanzas 20-21)

The syntactical inversions ("sways God nearby," "Blossomed Sarah") here are, as they usually are in *Homage* and the *Sonnets,* a heightening of language. (For an example of an awkward inversion, see stanza 3, "I summon, see, / from the centuries it.") The energy, the stops and starts, and the ellipses were by this time absorbed into Berryman's style.

Helen Vendler correctly feels that Berryman's stylistic development was in part a movement toward colloquial language; but she also finds that *Homage* was the first poem to arrive there.[20] The language of *Homage* is formal, archaic, biblical, elevated; it is seldom colloquial. A mixture of colloquial and formal language is much more apparent in the *Sonnets, The Dream Songs,* and *Love & Fame* than it is here.

Other reviewers have commented on the influence of Gerard Manley Hopkins on the style of *Homage*, noting the twists of syntax, the tendency toward the stanza as a unit, and the preponderance of heavily stressed syllables. Berryman's metrical practice in the poem is not really Hopkins's accentual system, a system that ignores the number of weakly stressed syllables in the line. Berryman's line does tend to have more heavy stresses than usual, but follows standard accentual-syllabic metrical patterns rather than Hopkins's. Berryman's account of the beginnings of the poem do not mention Hopkins. He credits the eight-line stanzaic pattern to his long study of Yeats, especially Yeats's "In Memory of Major Robert Gregory,"[21] but in *Homage* no distinctly Yeatsian influence is detectable. Metrically the stanza pattern is 5,5,3,4,5,5,-3,6; in Yeats's poem it was 5,5,5,4,5,4,4,5. The rhyming pattern of *Homage* is also considerably freer than Yeats's. The basic pattern (with the x indicating no rhyme) is *abxbccxa,* but there are many variations. It would be impossible to credit the many slant rhymes in the poem specifically to Yeats's influence; and Berryman experiments with rhymes that Yeats would probably have rejected as being too near the borders of non-rhyme. Examples are the mixture of masculine and feminine rhymes in "up-Winthrop" or the differing end consonant sounds in "waist-brace," a combination that some prosodists would call false rhyme.

Whatever its sources, the style of *Homage* is easily identifiable and thoroughly individualistic. The poem could not have been done as well by other poets, a criticism made by John Thompson of Berryman's early Yeats-Auden poems.[22] It is doubtful, however, that *Homage* is "the most distinguished long poem by an American since *The Waste Land,*" as Edmund Wilson wrote in a letter to the publishers. John Ciardi chides Wilson by reminding him of Hart Crane's *The Bridge* and Wallace Stevens's "Man with the Blue Guitar." Although generally praising *Homage,* Ciardi questions "whether the passion is . . . truly love . . . or more nearly a thing literary and made."[23] This atmosphere of artificiality is implied in Berryman's own account of the beginnings of *Homage:* ". . . When I finally woke up to the fact that I was involved in a long poem, one of my first thoughts was: Narrative! let's have narrative, and at least one dominant personality, and no fragmentation!—in short, let us have something spectacularly NOT *The Waste Land,* the best long poem of the age. . . . Maybe hostility keeps on going."[24] Berryman seems to have been writing more in literary rebellion than in self-expression.

The poet was unsure whether *Homage* belonged more to his early poetry or to his late. At one time, he said that until 1957 or so, he was "an utter bore"[25]; but in a Dream Song he says that he was nearly forty when he found his proper style and manner (Dream Song 369). *Homage* was completed when he was thirty-nine. It is by no means boring; and, by being a long poem in a highly original stanzaic form, it suggested the proper direction for the poet. Accordingly, Berryman began writing Dream Songs about a year after

Homage was published. But, at the same time, he was writing short poems that, with few exceptions, show no further expression of the poet's self.

VI   His Thought Made Pockets...

Berryman's haphazard development, his tendency to write in several styles at once, is seen in the eleven poems of *His Thought Made Pockets & the Plane Buckt* (1958). (The title is a line taken from Dream Song 5.) Only later did he acknowledge that what he called "long poems"—the *Sonnets, Homage,* and *The Dream Songs*—better suited his temperament. "I don't write short ones...," he said in 1969.[26] But, in spite of his relative success with the *Sonnets* and *Homage,* he wrote several short poems in the 1950's, and he wrote one (a maudlin elegy for John F. Kennedy) as late as 1963 ("Formal Elegy," *Short Poems,* 117-20).

The styles and themes of *His Thought Made Pockets* are as diverse as those of the early poems. Sometimes other poets intrude. Robert Frost's "A Considerable Speck" becomes Berryman's "They Have" (*Short Poems,* 104), as the poet observes two tiny insects crawling on his table and note-pad. Like Frost, he chooses not to let the creatures die. Ezra Pound seems to be lurking behind "Note to Wang Wei" (*Short Poems,* 114), a tribute to the Chinese poet-physician-painter of the eighth century. The title of three sociopolitical poems, "from *The Black Book,*" may have been borrowed from Thomas Middleton, who published his *Blacke Booke* in 1604. Middleton's allegorical narrative describes Lucifer's descent to London, his visits to brothels and the Royal Exchange, his encounters with various sinners. Berryman's poems are also devilish; they recount the sins of torture, rape, and murder the Nazis committed against the Jews. The third of the poems "from *The Black Book*" is powerfully sympathetic for the victims, sympathetic in a sincerity that Berryman could not achieve in the early poems that pitied the victims of American capitalism. The Jews here are given

> a little soap,
> disrobing, *Achtung!* in a dirty hope,
> they shuffle with their haircuts in to die.
> Lift them an elegy, poor you and I,
> fair & strengthless as seafoam
> under a deserted sky.
>
> (*Short Poems,* 109)

The scene is well evoked. The victims, their heads shaved, move in dazed helplessness from crowded railroad cars to the supposed shower room—the gas chamber. One word of command conveys the cold-bloodedness of the Nazis. The sky is "deserted" because no God is there. He could not be there, the poem seems to say, and still allow such things to happen.

"Venice, 182-" (*Short Poems,* 99) expresses the same despair at illicit love that we have noted in the *Sonnets:* ". . . we look at each other in entire despair, / her eyes are swimming by mine, and I swear / we àre in love." "Not to Live" (*Short Poems,* 111) is like *Homage* in recalling the difficult early years in an American colony; here, it is Jamestown, Virginia, the first permanent settlement in the New World. "The Mysteries" (*Short Poems,* 102) is seemingly spoken by a madman and is as opaque as the earlier poem "The Long Home."

The two best poems of *His Thought Made Pockets* are one of social commentary and one of personal statement. "American Lights, Seen from Off Abroad" (*Short Poems,* 112-13) praises Harry Truman and criticizes Dwight Eisenhower; it praises San Francisco for being individualistic and aloof, but it slashes many other American cities for materialism, gaudiness, racial prejudice, smugness, or the lost idealism of the early fathers. The poem is based loosely on the nursery rhyme "The Bells of London," which concludes "Here comes a candle to light you to bed, / Here comes a chopper to chop off your head." Berryman's version reads "Here comes a scandal to blight you to bed. / Here comes a cropper, That's what I said." ("To come a cropper" is to fail utterly.) In its theme, the loss of the American dream, "American Lights" is not unlike *Homage* or even earlier poems; but the free-wheeling, colloquial style anticipates future poems.

"The Poet's Final Instructions" might have been a Dream Song; it is arranged in three stanzas, although here of unequal length. In form, the poem is a modified sonnet (rhyming *abba, cdde,ffggcc*) with a basic pentameter line rather than the varied line lengths of Dream Songs. But the style, tone, and themes are those of many Dream Songs. The poet says that he is "Dog-tired," "suisired," and ready to be buried in 'Minneap," for, he claims,

> I couldn't rest from hell just anywhere. . . .
> Choiring & strange my pall!

I might not lie still in the waste of St Paul
or buy DAD's root beer. . . .

Drop here, with honour due, my trunk & brain
among the passioning of my countrymen
unable to read, rich, proud their tags
and proud of me. Assemble all my bags!
Bury me in a hole . . .
near Cedar on Lake Street, where the used cars live.

(*Short Poems,* 105)

The themes are social criticism and death. The style is Berryman in full stride. The colloquial "Dog-tired" contrasts with the formal "Choiring & strange my pall." The puns on "tags" and "bags" are ambiguously suggestive. The portmanteau word "suisired" could mean "self-born," "self-destroyed," or "'born of a father who killed himself." The tone of the poem is equally mixed: it has serious social criticism of America's anti-intellectualism and boosterism. There is the irony of the phrase "with honour due," the irony of insisting that Minneapolis is so much finer a place to be buried than St. Paul, and a larger irony when we recall the dead-serious final instructions given by men of the past. There is humor in "Minneap" and in the sign of "DAD's root beer" (an actual brand), until we recall "suisired." Finally, there is a concern about his own death almost hidden behind the energetic and zany goings-on of the poem. Technical control masquerading as off-handedness, sincerity mixed with irony, humor with sadness, elevation with deflation—these are qualities of the Dream Songs.

CHAPTER 4

The Major Poems: *The Dream Songs*

BERRYMAN had begun to write Dream Songs by 1956, and within three years they began to appear as individual poems in the *Times Literary Supplement*. The first group of them, divided into three books, was collected in *77 Dream Songs* (1964), a volume that won the Pulitzer Prize. The four books of *His Toy, His Dream, His Rest* (1968) completed the sequence and won the National Book Award. All seven books were combined in the volume *The Dream Songs* (1969), but several published Dream Songs were not collected in these volumes: one that introduces the *Sonnets,* one in *The Nation* (May 25, 1964), one in Life (July 21, 1967), three in *The Harvard Advocate* (Spring 1969), and surely others in various literary magazines. In addition, the poet composed many Dream Songs that were never printed; indeed, he said that he discarded more than fifty of them before *His Toy, His Dream, His Rest* was published,[1] and that he afterward wrote a dozen or more "just out of habit."[2] He considered *The Dream Songs* to be one long poem and excluded the uncollected poems from it; "none of them," he wrote, "will ever be attached to the poem by me, and in fact I may just leave them to be published after my death."[3]

I *The Coherence of* The Dream Songs

In an introductory note, the poet indicates that the protagonist and subject of *The Dream Songs* is an "imaginary character (not the poet, not me) named Henry, a white American in early middle age sometimes in blackface, who has suffered an irreversible loss and talks about himself sometimes in the first person, sometimes in the third, sometimes even in the second; he has a friend, never named, who addresses him as Mr Bones and variants thereof" (*The Dream Songs,* vi). Some of Henry's other names are Henry House, Henry Pussy-cat, and the Rabbi; and his unnamed friend might be named "cagey John" (51). The poet dons not only these masks but others in *The Dream Songs:* he is often a cat, once a racoon (57), an opossum (355), a deer (56), and, in one wild analogy, a helicopter (367). Whatever the masks, the informing personality of John Berryman is behind all of them, despite his tongue-in-cheek disclaimer in the introductory note. Henry is an "imaginary character" only in the sense that all characters are in literature — or, more exactly, in autobiography.

Berryman's assumption of different masks allows him to mix "tenderness and absurdity, pathos and hilarity that would have been impossible if the author had spoken in the first person."[4] The masks also allow Henry to express opinions that Berryman himself would never condone beyond a moment. For example, Henry's statement that we should bomb Red China (162) is a view that Berryman would almost certainly have been unwilling to state except as a passing thought born out of a sense of helplessness. Finally, the device of the masks permits Berryman largely, not entirely, to avoid the embarrassing revelations and the bathos of much confessional poetry of the past decade.

When he was asked to clarify the relationship of himself to Henry, Berryman said, "Henry does resemble me, and I resemble Henry; but on the other hand I am not Henry. You know, I pay income tax; Henry pays no income tax. And bats come over and they stall in my hair—and . . . I'm not Henry. Henry doesn't have any bats."[5] But in a Dream Song, Henry *is* described as a taxpayer; he notes that bats do not have problems with alcohol, banks, the law, or taxes; and he feels, therefore, that they "have it made. / Henry for joining the human race is *bats . . .*"(63). Berryman also freely admits the source of the name "Henry"; it was his second wife's pet name for him.[6] Henry, then, both is and is not Berryman.

The Dream Songs become the autobiography of a fragmented personality, unlike the *Prelude* of Wordsworth or the body of Yeats's poetry. In those works the writers had sorted out the elements of their personalities in such a way that they could see them as coherent. Berryman, in contrast, doubts the concept of a unified psyche; for, as he wrote in 1965, "I am less impressed than I used to be by the universal notion of a continuity of individual personality. . . ."[7] In answer to the question of why he called the Dream Songs one poem rather than a series of related lyrics, the poet remarked: "Ah—it's personality—it's Henry. He thought up all these things over all the years. The reason I call it one poem is the result of my strong disagreement with Eliot's line—the impersonality of poetry, an idea which he got partly from Keats (a letter) and partly from Goethe (again a letter). I'm very much against that; it seems to me on the contrary that poetry comes out of personality. . . . The placement of the poems in the *Dream Songs* is purely personal."[8] As Henry puts it, the "ultimate structure" of the poem is not that of carefully plotted melodrama; it is dependent only upon Henry's "nature" (293).

Several critics feel that *The Dream Songs* have no structure of any kind. William J. Martz states flatly that the volume "lacks plot, either traditional or associative."[9] Berryman responds by saying "Those are fighting words. It has a plot. Its plot is the personality of Henry as he moves on in the world. Henry gains ten years. At one time his age is given as forty-one . . . and at a later point he's fifty-one."[10] The poet is overstating his case by suggesting that the structure of the poem is chronological. That is true only in a very general sense; for, in the introductory note to *His Toy, His Dream, His Rest,* the poet has noted that some of the poems in that volume were written even before *77 Dream Songs* was published. And many poems deny a strictly chronological arrangement: for example, Dream Song 34 refers to Hemingway's death in 1961; Dream Song 40 is the poem in which Henry's age is given as forty-one, the poet's age in 1955. Other examples abound.

In a search for structure, the critic William Wasserstrom ingeniously discovered a close relationship between the four epigraphs to *77 Dream Songs.* The first, " 'THOU DREWEST NEAR IN THE DAY,' " is from Lamentations 3:57, which concludes with an injunction that Wasserstrom takes to be the dominant theme of *77 Dream Songs:* "FEAR NOT." The second epigraph, " 'GO IN, BRACK MAN, DE DAY'S YO' OWN.' " is also an epigraph to the standard history of the minstrel stage, Carl Wittke's *Tambo and Bones* (1930). The third epigraph is from Lamentations, as Berryman notes in the text; the fourth is from Olive Schreiner's *Dreams* (1914). Wasserstrom's argument is too complicated to paraphrase fully here, but the relationships he locates among the epigraphs make it clear that the poet was not working carelessly or haphazardly.[11]

Wasserstrom's idea that fear and the response to it are the important emotions in *77 Dream Songs* seems to be borne out by the first two epigraphs of *His Toy, His Dream, His Rest*. Both epigraphs are spoken by brave men who admitted their fear in face of great danger. The first, "NO INTERESTING PROJECT CAN BE EMBARKED ON WITHOUT FEAR. I SHALL BE SCARED TO DEATH HALF THE TIME," was said by Francis Chichester, the modern Britisher who sailed around the world alone. (One of the uncollected Dream Songs — in *Life*, [July 21, 1967] 74 — is in honor of Chichester.) The second epigraph is from Charles George Gordon, the British officer killed at Khartoum in 1885: "FOR MY PART I AM ALWAYS FRIGHTENED, AND VERY MUCH SO. I FEAR THE FUTURE OF ALL ENGAGEMENTS." But in *The Dream Songs*, fear is no more important than any number of other emotions. Wasserstrom's view that "fear not" is the dominant and structural theme is based only on the epigraphs. Berryman commented that Henry is "a hopeless coward with regard to his actual death. That never comes out in the poem, but he is afraid of death. I tried to make it clear in the epigraphs from Sir Francis Chichester and Gordon."[12] In a sense, then, the epigraphs are partly misleading in their emphasis on fear; for it is only one of Henry's many emotions in *The Dream Songs*.

In his search for a structural coherence, Wasserstrom also finds that in *77 Dream Songs* Berryman uses a pattern of numerical suggestiveness, "and thereby turn[s] the fact of number into a main issue within the very form of the verse. The 77 songs are distributed among three sections — 26, 25, 26. With nine exceptions, each poem is 18 lines in length, arranged in three verse paragraphs each six lines long. The nine exceptions must be deliberate, for Berryman resorts to the most patent subterfuges of dilation in order to vary a pattern which could easily conform to standard."[13] There is something to this argument, for *His Toy, His Dream, His Rest* is divided into four books of 308 Songs (308 is four times 77). The four books have, respectively, 13, 53, 132, and 106 Songs. We can note all kinds of mathematical possibilities: 13 is one-half of 26, 132 minus 106 is 26, 106 is twice 53, and so on. Other indications of the importance of magic numbers in *The Dream Songs* are such curiosities as listing the number wounded in the Charles Whitman mass slaying as thirty-three (Song 135), whereas the *Time* magazine article in which Berryman read about the case lists thirty-one.[14] I suspect, however, that the poet is toying with numbers rather than incorporating them in Dante's manner into an overall structure.

Berryman's view seems to be that the poetic personality behind a long poem is a sufficient organizing and unifying device. The view was stated most clearly by him in 1949 in his essay "The Poetry of Ezra Pound." Berryman feels that critics who attacked Pound's poetry were blinded to its subject—himself as a modern poet—because of their interest "in craft, not personality and subject. Also they have been blinded, perhaps, by the notion of the 'impersonality' of the poet. . . . For poetry of a certain mode (the dramatic) this is a piercing notion; for most other poetry, including Pound's, it is somewhat paradoxical, and may disfigure more than it enlightens." The reader is "baffled by a heterogeneity of matter . . . but he hears a personality in Pound's poetry." Berryman tries to refute the opinion that Pound's *Cantos* are only "a rag-bag" of the poet's interests, "a 'formless' work . . . 'not about anything' " by insisting that the *"Cantos* have always been personal; only the persona increasingly adopted . . . is Pound himself." Paradoxically, Berryman then says that "Pound too may really, like his critics, regard the work as nearly plotless and heroless" in any traditional sense.[15] This statement could be said also about *The Dream Songs*, but the question of the coherence of the Songs would not thereby be resolved for most readers, who would find both the *Cantos* and *The Dream Songs* lacking in a basic structure. The argument depends, finally, upon the definitions of the words "plot", "structure", and "coherence".

The Dream Songs are not in any case nonsensical ramblings. Many individual Songs are baffling only until we read the whole sequence, for the poems comment upon one another by repeated words and scenes. For example, Henry's two friends in Dream Song 365 are not there identified—an "old friend" asks an "older friend" why he does not come to visit him more frequently: the older friend replies, " 'I'm afraid you'll find me out.' " But the two speakers can be identified if we recall a line in Dream Song 39, the last of a series of three songs about Robert Frost: " 'Nobody' (Mark says you said) 'is ever found out.' "[16] Frost is the "old friend"; Mark Van Doren is the "older friend" since Berryman had known him longer. Similarly, Frost can be identified as the unnamed friend whom Henry visits at his "cabin" (218) by referring to a later Song in which Frost is named and the visit is again recalled (230). Occasionally a scene is repeated from the earlier works: Berryman's visit with Yeats in London, mentioned in Dream Songs 88 and 215, had first been presented in Sonnet 5, where Berryman compared his introduction to T. S. Eliot at Princeton in 1947 with his meeting the Irish poet a decade or so earlier at the old man's club, the Athenaeum.

Such repetitions give some continuity to Berryman's work, and sometimes they add to the meanings of a specific Dream Song. The meaning of the baffling word "Plop" (83, 84) is, for example, clarified in *Stephen Crane*. Berryman quotes the word from Crane's story "The Upturned Face," where it is used to describe the sound of earth falling into a grave (*Stephen Crane*, 257-58). One final example of a repetition is the image of a man climbing a tree. As we noted in Chapter Three, the image was, in "The Dispossessed" and in Sonnet 98, a symbolic equivalent of adultery. It is that also in Dream Song 350, where Henry predicts that there will have to be a law passed to keep him from "climbing trees, / & other people's wives. . . ." In Dream Song 1, the poet recalls climbing to the top of a "sycamore" where he sang out his joy, and surely the sycamore is the same one that he mounts in the *Sonnets*. In another Song he is an opossum in a tree and sexual activity of some kind is going on; he and the female are united, and the two of them together are said to be a " 'possum treed" (355). In Song 57, he is a different animal, and this time he is caught; he recalls a racoon treed, dogs barking, and "flashlights." Both the tree associated with adultery and the flashlights recur in Berryman's retelling in Dream Song 237 of the sensational Hall-Mills murder case of 1922.[17]

We shall note other interlocking phrases and images, but they too are insufficient in themselves to structure *The Dream Songs*. The themes of *The Dream Songs* are, however, the same as those of the earlier poetry—socio-political concerns, the nature of art and poetry, religious questions, friendship and love, dreams and psychological disorder, and, again, a sense of great loss. But to suggest a thematic coherence for *The Dream Songs* does not mean that all of them become clear—indeed, some of them are completely baffling. Nor does it mean that individual Songs have only one of these concerns; most of them jump from subject to subject with cheerful alacrity. Often a stanza in one Dream Song is more relevant to another Song than it is to the one in which it occurs. This quality in itself may be another reason Berryman insisted that the Dream Songs were one poem.

II *Social and Political*

Berryman's political stance in *The Dream Songs* is the same as in the earlier poetry—that of a white, middle-class, liberal intellectual. The sympathy for the underdog, the detestation of totalitarianism and of war, and the ambivalence toward America remain. But some of the villains and the victims have changed with the times. World War II is replaced by Vietnam; Communism supercedes Fascism as the most detested totalitarian force; the sympathy for exploited labor and for the Jews under Hitler changes to an empathy with Negroes. Sympathy for Jews is not, however, entirely absent from *The Dream Songs*. Henry calls himself an "imaginary Jew" (48) and compares himself to Leopold Bloom, the anti-hero of James Joyce's *Ulysses,* a "Hungarian Jew" (288); and, recalling the pogroms of the Nazis, Henry says that Germans are experts at killing (41). This sympathy for the downtrodden also extends to other peoples; Henry decries the slaughter of "the superior peoples"— "Armenians," "Jews," and "Ibos." (The Ibos are the major tribe in Biafra; in July 1968, their deaths from malnutrition were estimated at six thousand per day.) Henry adds that such massacres make it clear that civilization itself is only a stage of development that we have discarded in favor of "savagery" (353).

Berryman's empathy with Negroes is related directly to his awareness of the prejudice to which Jews are subjected. When asked why he employed Negro dialect in some Dream Songs, he replied,

Well, that's a tough question. . . . I wrote a story once called "The Imaginary Jew." I was in Union Square in New York, waiting to see my girl, and I was taken for a Jew (I had a beard at the time). There was a tough Irishman who wanted to beat me up, and I got into the conversation, and I couldn't convince them that I wasn't a Jew. Well, the Negro business—the blackface—is related to that. That is, I feel extremely lucky to be white, let me put it that way, so that I don't have that problem. Friends of mine—Ralph Ellison, for example . . . —he has the problem. He's black, and he and Fanny, wherever they go, they are black.[18]

But the poet's feelings for Negroes is not only the classic middle-class liberal's pity for downtrodden people who manage to survive; it is also an admiration of Negro achievements in art. I hesitate to say "folk-art" since that phrase carries connotations of condescension. Berryman admires Negroes for their creation of a dialect and a music—jazz and blues—that are highly original.

Only a few of the Dream Songs are entirely in Negro dialect. In one of these, Song 60, Henry angrily reminds his friend of the discrimination that Negroes encounter in America and how little has been done about it since the Supreme Court decision in 1954: "After eight years, be less dan eight percent, / distinguish' friend, of coloured wif de whites" in public schools in the South. Henry's friend points out that there are Negro sailors, some of them even officers; but Henry calls him an "Uncle Tom" and adds that whites keep most blacks "from de proper job, / de fairest houses & de churches eben." Henry's friend finally agrees that war between Negroes and "ofays" (white men, "foes" in pig-Latin) will probably result, and he wonders who will win. Henry replies that he does not know, "But I do guess mos peoples gonna *lose*." (The concluding two lines of the Song—"I never saw no pinkie wifout no hand. / O my, without no hand"—are in the rhythm of the blues, the rhythm followed throughout in Dream Song 40.) Given Henry's attitude about race prejudice in America, he is properly disgusted by the " 'white backlash' " (199), the peculiar rationalization during the 1960's that Negroes were moving too rapidly toward constitutionally guaranteed rights.

Although Berryman did not write about prejudice against Negroes until the Dream Songs, he once recalled that his interest in Negro language and music was present at least as early as his student days at Columbia when he listened to the blues records of Bessie Smith (mentioned in Song 68), Victoria Spivey, and Teddy Grace. (The last, not Victoria Spivey, furnished the fourth epigraph to *His Toy, His Dream, His Rest*.[19]) At some later time he became interested in the minstrel show and read Carl Wittke's *Tambo and Bones*.

The minstrel show devices of *The Dream Songs* are in themselves social commentary of a subtle kind. As Wittke explains, the minstrel shows developed from the performances of Thomas Dartmouth Rice in the 1820's. "Daddy" Rice dressed in ragged clothes, blacked his face with burnt cork, and danced to the nonsensical song "Jim Crow." Rice's popularity led eventually to the fullfledged minstrel show with many performers, one of whom was the "interlocutor," a white man without makeup who was something of a master of ceremonies. He was also the straight man for two

blackface comedians, "Tambo" and "Bones," named for the tam-
bourine and the bone castanets they played; and together they were
called the "endmen" because of their position on the stage. The interlocutor was formal and pompous; after he fed lines to the
endmen, the laughter was often at his expense.[20] Berryman has called Henry's friend the "interlocutor,"[21] but the friend seems always
to be in blackface and to speak in dialect. He is never, so far as I can
tell, a pompous white man.

Wittke tells us that one "favorite device of the endmen was to
entertain their audiences with the recital of a poem, or with a
speech, usually on a topic that was utterly nonsensical, and adorned
with puns galore."[22] Dream Song 2 is dedicated to "Daddy" Rice,
and it concludes with such an apparently nonsensical speech by Mr.
Bones: "—Hit's hard. Kinged or thinged, though, fling & wing. /
Poll-cats are coming, hurrah, hurray. / I votes in my hole." The
exact meaning is not clear, but the pun on "polecat" and the "hurrah,
hurray" (from the song "Dixie") are meant as attacks on a suppres-
sive social system. As William Wasserstrom says of the lines, "Sir
Bones speaks . . . a satiric language . . . devised in order to hide true
meaning from the Man, the enemy,"[23] the "ofay."

Henry can offer no new solutions to the Negro-white problem in
America. He sounds revolutionary at one point as he alters Marx-
ian phraseology—"Negroes, ignite! you have nothing to use but
your brains . . ." (232)—but he may mean simply that Negroes have
reservoirs of intelligence that remain untapped. His characteristic
view seems to be a wish for universal brotherhood rather than international revolution. In a Christmas poem he describes a snow that
falls for all men; the lawns are "white / with a heavy fall for ofays &
for dark," and the poet wants blacks and whites to express love for
one another in remembrance of Christ, "the Man who was not born
today . . ." (200).[24] Elsewhere he wishes that white rabbits and black
racoons could live in harmony, and he means not only animals
when he adds that he is certain that all creatures are "brothers"
(107).

Henry finds other things wrong in America besides racial prejudice. In Song 280, he is critical of American's "perpetual self-
laud," the view that this country is a soaring spirit and that all the
rest of the world is disgustingly verminlike and unimportant. In
Song 216, America's pride and presumptuousness are seen in the
stationing of regular troops in Europe and in having the U-2 spy

planes fly over Russia. Francis Gary Powers, the pilot of such a plane that was shot down in 1960, is despised first for admitting to the Russians his mission and then for returning to the United States as a celebrated hero.

Again, as in "American Lights, Seen from Off Abroad," America's self-congratulatory pride is found to be ironic in a land that can so easily forget its past. In Song 217, when Henry's students can hardly remember the Korean conflict, their dim recollections are called "unrecruited" both because the students have never been drafted and because they have difficulty gathering their thoughts. They are able to recall the Cuban invasion of 1961, and they have heard of Franklin Delano Roosevelt, but they seem vague about the time relationship of those phenomena. Henry is saddened by his own visions of the terrible battles of the Civil War and depressed by the students', and most Americans', lack of historical sense. Dream Song 22, "Of 1826," criticizes America for its anti-intellectualism, Dale Carnegie salesmanship, domineering women, and devotion to television. The last stanza mentions one important fact we have forgotten ("Collect" here means "prayer"): "Collect: . . . the dying man / . . . is gasping 'Thomas Jefferson still lives' / in vain. . . ." Berryman said in 1967 that "no national memory but ours could forget the fact that John Adams and Thomas Jefferson both died on the same day—the fourth of July in 1826."[25] Adams did make the remark "Thomas Jefferson still survives" as he lay on his death-bed.

Henry finds nuclear devices to be as frightening as Berryman had found them to be in "The Dispossessed"; he tries to hide from the threat of the hydrogen and atomic bomb (197). And, as in the earlier poems, war is a villain; Henry can hardly bear to think of men lost in battle. On a Memorial Day he is ironic and sad as he cheers for the dead soldiers (268). In Dream Song 226, the marines are subtly attacked for the deaths they have caused and sympathized with for the losses they suffer. Henry paraphrases the marine's catch-phrase of World War II (they fought "on the land, on the sea, and in the air"); he notes that many of the marines also "Disappeared" from the land, sea, and air; and he concludes that this world is "not a place to love"—a phrase that echoes and refutes a statement in Robert Frost's "Birches" that "Earth's the right place for love."

Henry considers the war in Vietnam to be even more detestable than World War II because the issues are amorphous. In Song 162, he is irritated that we have involved ourselves in an undeclared war in which the enemy is not ours but that of the South Vietnamese; and he remarks that it is impossible to distinguish who the South Vietnamese themselves are since the Viet Cong, the Communists in South Vietnam, are also the enemy. An end to the war is said to be as impossible to imagine as a sequel to Lewis Carroll's *Through the Looking Glass.* Henry rejects the notion that the war is a holy war of the united democracies against world Communism, insisting that our presence there directs all our allies. He mourns all lives lost in the conflict, not only combatants', and mentions the several Buddhists who have committed suicide in protest against the government of South Vietnam.

Similarly, Dream Song 66 is Henry's reaction to the death of a Buddhist monk who killed himself by having fellow monks pour gasoline over him and then setting himself aflame. Perhaps irresponsibly, Henry accuses the United States government of being unmoved by such protests and invents a new cabinet member—or borrows the title held by British cabinet minister John Profumo—a "Secretary of State for War" who shrugs off such incidents and then engages "a redhaired whore." Berryman himself expressed a distaste for poets who try to capitalize on the war;[26] and when Henry goes on a reading tour to raise money to aid Vietnam (169), he probably is referring to his tax money that goes to support the war. He complains about "shelling taxes" out in Song 201, punningly reminding us that tax money buys shells.

Another villain has superseded the capitalists of the early verse. Now, if anyone is to be blamed for America's difficulties of the 1950's and 1960's, it is politicians and bureaucrats. Especially disliked is Dwight Eisenhower, who is called "ignorant"(216) and is viciously scored in a Dream Song that parodies his speech patterns, his campaign slogan, and his ideas:

> we—I like—
> at the Point he was already terrific—sick
>
> to a second term, having done no wrong—
> no right—no right—having let the Army—bang—
> defend itself from Joe, let venom' Strauss
> bile Oppenheimer out of use—use Robb,

who'll later fend for Goldfine—Breaking no laws,
he lay in the White House—sob!!—

who never understood his own strategy—whee—
so Monty's memoirs—nor any strategy,
wanting the ball bulled thro' all parts of the line
at once—proving, by his refusal to take Berlin,
he misread even Clauswitz—wide empty grin
that never lost a vote (O Adlai mine).

                                                                                        (23)

"Joe" is Joseph McCarthy, leader of the anti-Communist witch-hunts of the early 1950's. "Strauss" and "Robb" were instrumental in the 1954 denial of security clearance to Robert Oppenheimer, the scientist in charge of the development of the atom bomb in New Mexico during World War II. According to the poem, Roger Robb was also involved with Bernard Goldfine in a scandal (the "vicuna coat" scandal) during Eisenhower's administration. "Monty" is British Field Marshal Bernard Montgomery, who in his memoirs claimed that Eisenhower's direction of the Allied invasion of Europe on D-Day, June 6, 1944, was inept. Berryman compares that ineptness with Eisenhower's aggressive football playing when he was a cadet at West Point. Karl von Clausewitz (1780-1831) wrote *On War,* the first book that promulgated the theory of total war—war against civilian as well as military objectives. Eisenhower's permitting the Russians to take Berlin, a move designed to save American lives, resulted of course in a divided Germany and Berlin. "Adlai" Stevenson, liberal Democrat who ran against Eisenhower unsuccessfully in two presidential campaigns, is the kind of politician Berryman favored—urbane, articulate, and above all an intellectual. In 1969, after Stevenson's death, Eugene McCarthy and Nelson Rockefeller were his political heroes.[27]

The admiration expressed for John F. Kennedy in "Formal Elegy"—"He seemed good: / brainy in riot, daring, cool" (*Short Poems,* 120)—is modified in Song 245, "A Wake-Song," although Kennedy himself is not attacked so much as the government officials who surrounded him. They are called "fools"—some of them "sur-" fools (superfools)—because of their supervisory positions and supreme foolishness; others are "sub-fools" because of their position as underlings and because they are excessively stupid. All are said to be incompetent yes-men, all spy on one another, and all are supervised by an administrator from the Ivy League. Kennedy's executive assistants are scored no more than certain members of Congress (one is an easily recognized Representative from Harlem) who make cynical appeals to the American populace. It seems that Lyndon Johnson, Kennedy's Vice-President and successor, is excluded from this attack. Johnson had been praised for his wisdom in "Formal Elegy" (*Short Poems,* 120), and Henry's respect for him has not declined; in Song 354, Johnson is called "generous" and "able." This view seems contradictory to Henry's attitude toward the war in Vietnam, for which Johnson must accept much of the responsibility.

At times, Henry's complaints against the government are simply petty, as when he rants about the infrequency of mail delivery, wondering why we cannot make the Postmaster General (called a "Cabinet jerk") see to it that mail is delivered at least as often as it was in Paris or London during the nineteenth century, or as often as it was in Oklahoma during the poet's boyhood, when he enjoyed "three and four deliveries" daily. Ironically, the mail Henry does receive is not particularly welcome—newspapers filled with gloomy news, and communiqués from his bank, his insurance companies, and his lawyers (167).

If Henry finds much wrong with America, he finds more wrong elsewhere. The Pakistanis and the Sudanese are said to govern themselves even more poorly than the Americans (31). Russians are worse; Henry reminds Nikita Khrushchev that he is no better than Stalin was, and that he too must someday die (59); and Lenin is called simply a "criminal" (363). The lack of artistic freedom in Russia is mourned by Henry as he recalls the trial of a young Russian poet and translator, Joseph Brodsky, who was sentenced to five years at hard labor for supposed political crimes (180-181).

In spite of his attacks on America, Henry can at times be patriotic. In Ireland, the raising of the American flag at the embassy every morning stirs him to say that he is shamelessly patriotic (339). He becomes defensive about America when, in India, he is questioned about racial prejudice in his country; and, although irritated, he does not point out to his audience that the Indian caste system is based upon skin color (24). Clearly, Henry loves his country despite its failings. Only once does he praise another governmental system; he finds Scandinavians in general and Swedes in particular to be supremely capable of self-government. He says that they simply "don't exist" (31) because he can hardly believe the enviable balance of orderliness and freedom that characterizes Scandinavian societies, and because he knows that American society is unlikely to achieve such a balance.

Henry's contradictory feelings about his country and its political system are those shared by most liberal intellectuals. Frequently they are ambivalent toward the concept of democracy: they believe in the basic equality of men but at the same time distrust the unthinking mob. Berryman expresses this view in a recounting of two incidents, one that occurred when he was teaching at Harvard in the early 1940's, the other some time later. He claims that even as a child he, like Winston Churchill, knew of no suitable alternative to democracy; therefore, he tried it at Harvard by allowing his class of freshmen to vote on the one long novel they would read during the semester. They selected Margaret Mitchell's *Gone With the Wind;* Berryman, or Henry, exercised his veto and the class was required to read Leo Tolstoy's *War and Peace.* Later, apparently at Princeton, when Berryman and his grading assistant were discussing politics, the graduate student, who was working toward his doctorate in political science, admitted that he believed a monarchy to be the best of all political systems. Henry is equally disgusted by the failure of democracy and by the supposed intellectual who believes in kingship; he distrusts both the judgments of the mob and of the intellegentsia. But Henry concludes this poem by saying that even a monarcy might be preferable to allowing a "few mindless votes" of the sort that resulted in the brothers of John F. Kennedy being elected to public office (105).[28] As usual, Henry seems torn between several alternative positions, all of which seem to him untenable.

If Henry's political views are inconsistent, we must recall that Berryman refused to identify himself with his created character and hence could insist that none of Henry's views were necessarily shared by the poet. Surely, though, every view that Henry expresses was held at some time by Berryman. One reason Henry's creator preferred not to call his poetry autobiographical was that he was trying to allow for the "drift-of-life,"[29] the expression of tentative views as well as permanent ones, the right to hold opinions sometimes only momentarily. The result is some contradiction and confusion, but this may be the characteristic attitude of thinking men during this age of anxiety.

Undeniably, Henry's political views frequently seem naive;

sometimes they seem unfair, as in the attack on Eisenhower. But Henry has at least managed to avoid the pitfalls of Pound, who broadcast Fascist propaganda during World War II, or of Yeats, who joined an Irish Fascist organization in the 1930's. Fortunately, Henry and Berryman never traveled in the reactionary direction that Robert Frost once predicted for young liberals who grow older.

III *The Art of Poetry*

Henry's musings sometimes return to the nature of art and particularly of poetry. As in "Winter Landscape," the permanence of art is its primary quality — its ability to escape time. Henry finds that quality in the work of Goya (331), Mozart, Bach (157), Schubert (258), and other artists and composers, but most often in the art of poetry. Like Milton or Joyce, Henry finds writing to be a high calling, a vocation that first requires a sense of others' achievements in it. Henry's admiration includes Dante (279), Ben Jonson (126), Keats (190), and Whitman (279); but he dwells most upon modern writers. Among them are Yeats, Thomas, Eliot, Pound, Frost, and Robert Lowell, all of whom Henry has met or known:

> Fortune gave him to know the flaming best,
> expression's kings in his time, by voice & hand,—
> the Irishman,
> the doomed bard roaring down the thirsty west,
> the subtle American British banker-man
> and the lunatic one
>
> fidgeting, with bananas, and his friend the sage
> (touchy, 'I'm very touchy') in his cabin
> two miles from mine here,
> and already now let's call it a strong age,
> not just a science age . . .;
>
>   I add on the Bostonian,
> rugged & grand & sorrowful.
>
>   (218)

There are many others whom Henry admires and praises—Synge and Joyce (290), Hemingway and Faulkner (39), William Carlos

Williams (324), Theodore Roethke (18), Delmore Schwartz, Rolfe
Humphries (291), Randall Jarrell. Henry is able to praise a few
women poets—Sappho, Emily Dickinson, Emily Brontë, Marianne
Moore, Elizabeth Bishop, Sylvia Plath (187), and Adrienne Rich
(362). (Noticeably, he excludes Anne Bradstreet from this list; in
The Dream Songs Henry refers to her only obliquely in a reference
to *Homage* [75].) But he is not averse to being savage with writers
who, in his opinion, failed to succeed; for example, the eighteenth-
century poet James Thomson is called "boring" (231). Coleridge,
Poe, and Rilke "shout commands" that Henry refuses to hear,
perhaps some abstract nonsense about the Imagination (12). The
modern Irishmen Patrick Kavanaugh and Austin Clarke are said to
have an audience who can hardly read poetry at all (321). An unnamed former student of Henry's will, in his opinion, never be an
accomplished or famous poet (98).

Henry repeats from *Homage* the notion that writers in our time
must feel themselves to be exiles. He calls R. P. Blackmur, Randall
Jarrell, and Delmore Schwartz "freaks" (282), but Henry does not in-
tend to be derogatory but factual. There is similarly "something
bizarre about Henry . . . / unlike you & you . . ." (78). Henry works
in exile even from his friends and his wife (280); surrounded by his
family, he still feels as "isolated" as a household pet (260).
Although he does not really like his isolation (28), it seems to be
necessary for the creation of poetry. Artists are, then, different from
the common run of mankind; they form something of a "clan" (88)
or a priesthood (73). The aspirant must meet certain qualifications
before he can join this select fraternity. Henry says that the subject
matter and the techniques of poetry have long been established and
that, in days of yore, "tests really tests" were devised and judged by
the "masters" (125). He complains that now, however, the initiation lacks formality and high seriousness. He describes the
neophytes in a college creative writing class, perhaps the one
Berryman taught at the State University of Iowa in 1954.[30] The
students do not have to suffer to learn their craft; and they have
"unlimited time" to qualify for the profession, simply by waiting
until *Poetry* magazine admits them. Meanwhile, they are dressed
casually; and most of them view the process of poetry more as
"fun" than as a demanding vocation. Henry himself goes through
his own hasty initiation in Song 229, with the laying on of hands of
the impatient masters who rush him through "the major & minor

orders" and, in a parody of a meaningful ritual, tell him " 'You're in business.' " Henry's slangy response to such a slapdash ceremony is wholly appropriate; he says only *" 'OW.' "*

Henry's view that poetry is a kind of priesthood accounts for the absolute inexplicability of some of the Dream Songs. If he is serving a religious function, he has no responsibility to be clear. A passage in Berryman's *Stephen Crane* paraphrases a theory of poetry and explains Henry's method: [31]

Robert Graves . . . laid out a theory of the origin of poetry once. A savage dreams, is frightened by the dream, and goes to the medicine man to have it explained. The medicine man can make up anything, anything will reassure the savage, so long as the manner of its delivery is impressive; so he chants, perhaps he stamps his foot, people like rhythm, what he says becomes rhythmical, people like to hear things *again,* and what he says begins to rhyme. Poetry begins—as a practical matter, for *use.* It reassures the savage. Perhaps he only hears back again, chanted, the dream he just told the medicine man, but he is reassured; it is like a spell. And medicine men are shrewd: interpretation enters the chanting, symbols are developed and connected, the gods are invoked, poetry booms.

(*Stephen Crane,* 273)

Henry's friend asks him once whether he has been to see such a "medicine man" (366), but Henry himself is at times the savage priest. When Henry's friend says, "You don' make sense," Henry's response is "—I don't try to. Get with it" (272). Henry insists later that his poems are not intended "to be understood, you understand. / They are only meant to terrify & comfort" (366).

Henry is, then, a priest of sorts; but he can also be at times a veritable God. " 'Tetelestai' " ("It is finished"), he says to conclude Song 354, speaking Christ's last words. A "makar" (an archaic Scottish word for "poet") is compared to God in Song 94. Berryman only infrequently makes this comparison of the poet to a Creator, a comparison Dylan Thomas regularly insists upon; but the analogy strengthens Henry's view that art has a religious function. A concomitant of the theory that art serves such a high purpose has often been the notion that art is ultimate reality, but Berryman refreshingly makes no such claim for poetry. It is one reality, but others exist alongside it.

The *" 'OW' "* that Henry exclaimed at his initiation was not entirely humorous, for he also sees art as a painful process for its prac-

titioners. In Song 258, he sympathizes with the unhappy careers of r
Scarlatti, Mozart, and Schubert, difficult lives that somehow ᵈ
resulted in the production of art. Henry's pain in creating art is ˢ
similar to theirs; it is once compared to that of an operation, sur- ¹
gery that he is compelled to perform upon himself (67). And, in
order to give life to his poetry, he is obliged to give up his own,
offering up to us his "blood in pawn" (175), echoing Dylan
Thomas's theme of the poet's blood flowing from himself into his
poetry.

The poet's suffering seems to be necessary to art; but, if he suffers, he also causes pain to his readers in the sense that he stirs them
deeply. His function is in part, "to wound," a quality that Henry
finds lacking in Wallace Stevens's poetry (219). Henry also feels
that poetry has another purpose—"to make laugh" (271); and these
poems are successful in that intent. Although Berryman always admired humor in other poets—in 1948 he praised Henry Reed's
"Lessons of the War" particularly for that quality [32]—he seemed, in
his early poems, virtually incapable of it himself. *The Dream Songs*
capitalize on the outrageous humor we find only occasionally in the
Sonnets and in *His Thought Made Pockets*.

An artist, then, is a man who must suffer to create; but the
reward is great—fame. Although not of noble mind, Henry is
enamoured of fame and speculates about it often. Once he wonders
what constitutes it. Is it seeing "parodies" or "imitations" or "trans-
lations" of one's own work? Is it the winning of all the important poetry prizes? Is it a newspaper notice, an interview on television or radio,
appreciative letters from foreigners? Henry is uncertain and concludes that a single letter from a young admirer is the most rewarding
proof that a poet has become famous (342). But Henry also longs for
that larger fame, for being known and read by many people; and he is
convinced at times that he has achieved it. He says that he is now a
"Big One," and is amazed that he does not feel himself to be different
from what he ever was (7). Even at these times, Henry, eternally the
idealist disillusioned, cannot realize why fame does not bring him
contentment (133). Typically, Henry is contented least with what he
most enjoys, and longs for a privacy that fame does not allow, expressing a desire "for a middle zone" where he could be famous and
still retain a modicum of privacy (287). Later in *The Dream Songs*
Henry accepts fame—and the slight monetary rewards it brings to
poets—as his proper due: *"Such* hard work demands such inter-

national thanks / besides better relations with one's various banks"
340).

   Characteristically confused, Henry is not always certain that he is
a poet or that, even if he has found fame, he is successful in his art.
He insists that artists must eternally "fear" that they may not be artists at all (125); and, in a moment of despair, he says that he has
"Failed as a makar" (184). More often he seems confident of
success, as when he compares himself to Winston Churchill, in
Song 323. First he notes their slight differences—Churchill was
energetic and gleeful, while Henry is "inactive" and subject to anxiety—but their similarities are more important: both drank excessively (Churchill is said to have consumed a pint or more of
brandy daily); both were master stylists; both were able to think
"on their feet"; both were not successful or famous until late in life.
(Henry is recalling Churchill's embarrassing defeat, as First Lord of
the Admiralty, in the Dardanelles campaign during World War I.
Churchill was a victorious leader, finally, in World War II.) Henry
asks us to watch, now, to see what will happen to him, and the implication is that he will be as successful in poetry as Churchill had
been in statesmanship. That also is the tone of Dream Song 87,
perhaps the fairest representative of Berryman's view of his achievement. This Song is one of the several in which Henry is figured as
dead; he is rumored to be returning to this life ("to the foothills of
the cult") where he will walk triumphantly along "the lower slopes"
of Mount Parnassus. Henry seems certain of his success but is willing to admit that his is not the high poetry of a Milton or a Dante.

   Whatever the level of his achievement, Henry fears that the artist's dedication to his craft means that he cannot succeed in other
areas. Henry feels a sense of conflict between his life as a poet and his
other responsibilities, domestic and academic. The domestic conflicts occur infrequently and seem temporary (257), perhaps
because Henry feels guilty if he does not meet his obligations as
husband and father. Although he warns both men and women that
poets are not by nature domesticated, and make poor husbands or
wives (187), he has no sympathy with writers who, like Emerson,
neglected their wives for their work (294).

   Henry's conflict with academia seems to be a persistent one. He
recalls another poet-professor, Gerard Manley Hopkins, who in
Henry's view wasted himself by teaching Classics at Cambridge
(206). Henry can hardly bear to meet his own classes (134), but he

feels a responsibility to do so (274). After he has done his best for his students, he is irritated by those who have made no notes and have not been moved by his performance; he compares his feeling at such times to being kicked in the face (254). As he approaches sabbatical year in Ireland, he knows that the conflict between art and expediency is nearing a climax; once, entering his classroom and noticing two chairs left on the podium by a careless janitor, he angrily hurls them to the floor, shocking his students (275). He longs for the time when he will have "only the actual" work of poetry (297). As Berryman commented elsewhere, "To write is hard and takes the whole mind and wants one's whole time; a university is the perfect place not to write."[33] When asked how he viewed his role as a teacher in relation to his poetry, he replied, "There's no connection. Teaching keeps my relations with my bank going. Otherwise they would be very stuffy with me."[34]

Henry's distaste for the academic world is not limited to his teaching duties. He dislikes the factionalism that universities are subject to (278), the importance placed on service and technical courses (278), the hierarchical rank structure of university faculties, and the emphasis upon criticism and scholarship rather than upon poetry itself. Henry wonders whether college teachers will be promoted by writing articles about his poetry (373). In Song 308, "An Instructions [sic] to Critics," he advises them not to attempt to analyze The Dream Songs, saying that they would do better to remember the pretty girls they have kissed.

The academic scene is satirized in "MLA," Dream Song 35, in which the poet drunkenly describes a convention of college teachers in Washington D.C.; watches them as the men eye a professor's wife named Mary; and belittles the academic production of scholarly works:

> . . . all of you did theses or are doing
> and the moral history of what we were up to
> thrives in Sir Wilson's hands—
> who I don't see here—only deals go screwing
> some of you out, some up—the chairmen too
> are nervous, little friends—
>
> a chairman's not a chairman, son, forever,
> and hurts with his appointments; ha, but circle— . . .
> though maybe Frost is dying—around Mary;

> forget your footnotes on the old gentleman;
> dance around Mary.

MLA, the Modern Language Association, is made up of teachers of literature and languages. The annual Christmas convention is noted more as a place to look for a new job or to attend publishers' parties than for the quality of its literary discussions. Berryman satirizes especially the pedantry of "theses" or dissertations; and he implies that a series of editions of American authors, editions sponsored by the MLA, is also pedantry. He sides with "Sir Wilson," Edmund Wilson, who has attacked the editions.

Henry views literary criticism—or at least most of it—as non-art and as clearly subordinate to poetry. He has asked us to forget footnotes, for they are, he says, of interest only to graduate students (352). Criticism is thoroughly deflated in Song 170:

> —I can't read any more of this Rich Critical Prose,
> he growled, broke wind, and scratched himself & left
> that fragrant area.
> When the mind dies it exudes rich critical prose. . . .

Henry seems to have more respect for scholarship than for literary criticism. He recalls one of his own scholarly endeavors—studying the letters of John Keats at the Morgan Library—and brags that, as a scholar, he sometimes finds it necessary to correct "his betters / as well as his lessers & and would have had to say / much but for his different profession" (364). Henry does not mention the many scholarly works that his creator has produced in fields as widely separated as the Elizabethan age, the eighteenth century, and the present. But, however interesting scholarship is and however adept Henry is at it, his profession of poetry makes it only an avocation.

We must remember that Berryman himself produced both criticism and scholarship and had only respect for such writings when they were done well—as done, say, by A. E. Housman (206) or by Edmund Wilson. But Henry's view generally seems to be Berryman's when he compares *Homage to Mistress Bradstreet* to a flourishing tree and the critics of that poem to mangy dogs who sniffed around and then urinated on it (75). The critics are called "bare" in contrast to the green tree; the tree here, like Yeats's "great-rooted blossomer" in "Among School Children," sym-

bolizes an achieved organic unity. Clearly, Berryman agreed with
Matthew Arnold that poetry and criticism are not equally imaginative and creative.

IV *Religious Attitudes*

Although Henry finds a religious function in his art, he does not
thereby discard religion itself. Unlike James Joyce, Henry feels a
need for religious values apart from his aesthetic attitudes. At one
time or another he asks most of the important religious questions:
Does God exist? If so, what are His attributes? Does the universe
follow some kind of plan? Does man have an immortal soul? The
answers Henry finds are never simple and frequently vary.

Once, Henry indirectly questions the existence of God. Henry is
seen in blackface, "waiting upon the Lord" (in the sense of awaiting
his arrival rather than serving Him); suddenly Pascal appears, and
he and Henry begin to place "cagey bets" (232). The allusion is to
the *Pensées* of that seventeenth-century Christian apologist,
specifically to a section entitled "Of the Necessity of the Wager."
The issue there is whether God exists, an issue that, Pascal insists,
cannot be settled by reason. But man is "forced to wager"; he is "not
free" to avoid placing the bet one way or the other—"It is not option-
al." Pascal argues that it would be foolish not to wager that God exists
since so much is thereby to be gained and nothing to be lost. The alternative, to wager that God does not exist, would be unwise, because
of the possible consequences.[35] In his Song, Henry at first seems to be
involved in placing a bet, but he concludes with a denial of the view
that man is forced to make the wager at all; he is "free & loose." Henry is here, then, unwilling to assert either God's existence or nonexis-
tence, taking the position of an agnostic.

But agnosticism is not Henry's characteristic view. At times, he
assents to Christ's goodness and implies His divinity. A Christmas
poem finds the poet alongside a tree like the cross, "whereon he
really hung, for you & me" (200). Song 234, "The Carpenter's
Son," repeats Christ's message, "—Repent, & love," and the poet
says, "Pass me a cookie," the Eucharist wafer. God is called
"substantial" (94) and must therefore exist in one form or another.

Henry seldom, then, doubts God's existence; but, as in *Homage*
or in the third poem "from *The Black Book*," he often questions the
attributes traditionally assigned to God—absolute justice, mercy,
love, omnipresence, omniscience, and so on. In "Kyrie Eleison,"

Song 174, Henry agrees that God's duties are difficult ones; He is described as a supreme physicist, a miraculous maker of snow, a family counselor, and a busy judge who not only sorts out evil souls from the good but also sees that the good are rewarded. Henry complains, however, that while God busies himself with cataloguing "the bloody saints," Henry is left feeling lost and alienated. God seems to be somewhere "abroad" rather than here, where He is needed (94). Again, as in "from *The Black Book,*" Henry doubts that God could be present in this world when such terrible things happen in it. Henry imagines himself, but not God, to be present when the Reverend Hall and Mrs. Mills were viciously murdered; but, when those two lovers arrived in heaven and sang God's praises, "Henry was not there" (237) because he refuses to praise a creature who allows evil to occur. Instead, he is sardonic, saying that his own experience has not resulted in a belief that God is concerned for man; God's "love must be a very strange thing indeed, / considering its products" (256).

Henry is attempting to resolve the paradox called the Problem of Evil: How can evil exist in a world created by a God who is perfectly good, omnipotent, and omnipresent? There are many ways of resolving the paradox—perhaps evil does not exist or is only apparent evil, perhaps God does not exist, perhaps the evil is part of an overall structure that man cannot comprehend. Henry chooses none of these solutions; instead, he again questions God's attributes themselves. Perhaps God is not omnipresent or onmiscient, or

> Perhaps God is a slob,
> playful, vast, rough-hewn.
>
> Perhaps God resembles one of the last etchings of Goya. . . .
> Something disturbed,
> ill-pleased, & with a touch of paranoia
> who calls for this thud of love from his creatures-O.
> Perhaps God ought to be curbed.
>
> (238)

Less humorously, Henry says that God must be a haphazard beast; but Henry has a "divided soul" (317) on the matter of God's qualities. He may question them, but he is never willing to reject God or to curse Him and die.

Henry's religious views are deeply felt and highly personal ones.

Although he has assisted at Mass as an altar boy (129), dislikes rushing through religious services (336), and observes the feast days of his favorite saints (47, 255), his religious feelings are frequently unorthodox. He finds God's representatives on earth, the priests and theologians, to be largely ignorant, although he admits that they do their best (174). A distaste for theological disputation itself is implied in the several disrespectful references to Jesuits, the Catholic order most noted for its adeptness at fielding religious questions. (When his daughter was born, "The parking lot tilted & made a dance, / ditching Jesuits" [186]).

Henry is an unorthodox Christian also in his response to the other religions of the world. He stands before the statue of Buddha in the meditation garden at Kyoto and responds with fervor (73); he finds refuge from evil not only in the Catholic Brother Martin de Porres but also in the Eastern Orthodox Saint Simeon, the Jewish Baal-Schem-Tov, and the Bodhidharma of Buddhism (17). Henry seems to have found many of his religious sympathies in one of the courses Berryman teaches at Minnesota, a course in the "high religions—Christianity and Buddhism."[36]

In his views of the afterlife, Henry is most unorthodox, perhaps even heretical. Friends now dead are usually referred to as ghosts, and they seem to have an existence only in Henry's memory (146, 127) or in the mouldy grave itself (42, 61, 244, 324), or in a shadowy underworld similar to that in Greek mythology (21). Again, Henry is unwilling to be certain; he speculates that at his own projected death God may return to earth to rescue him, or he may simply vanish (220)—he is not sure which. Most references to the afterlife are humorously disbelieving, as when Henry claims that the traditional concepts of heaven describe a locale that would be endlessly boring since there would be no "occupation" there except praising God (256). God's process of selection for such a place is humorously called "hiring or firing" (286). Since Henry is sometimes a coward, he repeats the view of hell that he had been taught as a child—that the torments there will be immeasurably more painful than any suffering man undergoes in this life (353); but he suggests in the next lines of this Song that good people may simply escape from all conscious existence and "sleep forever" rather than serve in a heavenly choir.

Henry's most consistent view of the afterlife seems, however, to be that death is a casket from which no one escapes either in body or soul (196). He views the arguments about the immortality of the soul as one of those theological questions insoluble in this life, and has only wry words for those who believed that they had the answer to the question of immortality—Pascal, Spinoza, Saint Augustine, and Mary Baker Eddy, the founder of Christian Science who, according to Song 347, had a telephone line installed in her crypt so that she could maintain communication with her newspaper, the *Christian Science Monitor*. Henry notes that the telephone has not yet rung, and neither "has Christ returned," as so many Christians, early and late, expected. Henry says that, in any case, he wants release from his torment while on earth, not in an afterlife (256). His view is the Existential one that man's hell or heaven is available to him in this life; and he seems to have a share of each. Life is sometimes the Sartrean hell of the present (57), but Henry finds also that heaven exists here and now in his own Minneapolis (119).

Such heresy is supported at times by Henry's insistence that he is unrepentant; he says that he prefers the season of fall and is ready to exist eternally in "a world of Fall" (77), and he means man's fall as well as the season of the year. But Henry turns out to be not so heretical. He believes, with Anne Bradstreet, that his body is punished in order to give pleasure to his soul. He suffers from many physical infirmities—broken bones and intestinal disorders, for example—and considers them God's judgments upon a very un-Joblike creature (113). Henry is unwilling to extend God's punishment of man in this life into an afterlife and reasonably pleads that He can hardly find Henry guilty; he asks the court of the final judgment to allow him to enter a plea that he is "Not Guilty by reason of death" (86), a plea that may be heretical but one which strikes a note that most men have sung at one time or another. Death is in itself sufficient punishment for man's behavior in this life.

Henry's individualistic Christian ideas are not intended as rebellion, but as honest expressions of his beliefs. He is not really comfortable, however, in his conflicts with Catholicism and seems to wish for a closer relationship than the one permitted him by his heretical views—and by his two divorces. Dream Song 55 presents the poet's applying to the Church as if he were being interviewed for a position in it. But, Henry says,

Peter's not friendly. He gives me sideways looks. . . .
A pity,—the interview began so well. . . .

I feel my application failing. It's growing dark,
some other sound is overcoming. His last words are:
'We betrayed me.'

Clearly Henry feels that Peter has made it impossible for their conflict to be resolved; the Church, as well as Henry, is blamed for the
betrayal of Christ.

Perhaps one Song best summarizes Henry's mixture of
traditional and personal religious attitudes:

Dinch me, dark God, having smoked me out.
Let Henry's ails fail, pennies on his eyes . . . ,
                    drunkard & Boy Scout. . . .

          Was then the thing all planned?
I mention what I do not understand. . . .
God loves his creatures when ne treats them so?
Surely one grand *exception* here below
his presidency of

the widespread galaxies might once be made
for perishing Henry, whom let not then die.
He can advance no claim,
save that he studied thy Word & grew afraid,
work & fear be the basis for his terrible cry
not to forget his name.

(266)

"Dinch" is a verb formed from the slang word "dincher," a
cigarette; "to 'dinch' a cigarette is to stub it out."[37] God has
"smoked" Henry out both in the sense that he has found him out
and that he has used him for His own purposes, however obscure.
Henry's eyes will remain forever closed, in his grave. He is both
good and evil, "drunkard & Boy Scout," and knows that his body
will return only to the soil. He does not understand this life and
cannot resolve the problem of evil; if God has a plan for the universe, Henry cannot puzzle it out; but he pleads for a kind of immortality, a name that will be remembered. The plea is a wish for

fame rather than for an existence in an afterlife of any sort. The poet suggests that, because he has studied God's "Word," worked at his vocation, and is afraid of death, his plea is not unreasonable.

Henry is essentially a religious man; the tone of this last Song is humble and properly respectful. Althouth some of the other Songs present a Henry who is unregenerate, he can by no means be said to have "abandoned" his faith, a judgment made by William J. Martz about the early Berryman.[38] Rather, he is a man questing for religious beliefs, finding some, and refusing to submit when he cannot follow orthodoxy. I am reminded here of Wallace Stevens's "Sunday Morning" in which theological attitudes were expressed that once were anathema to Christianity but have become accepted in recent years by growing numbers of theologians.

V   *Friendship and Love*

"The universe has gifted me with friends . . . ," Henry says (360), and friendship and love are important values for him. Many of the Dream Songs are dedicated to the poet's literary, medical, or personal friends, but often no apparent connection exists between the person and the Song dedicated to him. Several Songs are in direct praise of such friends; an example is Song 304, which mentions the first names of some of them—"Maris," "Valerie," "Ellen," "Boyd," and "Phil." These people and others can be identified—at least we can learn their last names—by referring to the poet's dedicatory note to the *The Dream Songs;* but such poems (and there are many of them in the volume) seem to me more suited to private correspondence than to public poetry. This kind of Song is even less satisfactory when the friend is not named—a young lady in 358 and 375, an attractive woman in 360, and so on. Given Henry's usual frankness, perhaps he should have told us who these are. Or, if he feels that the situation is too private to be exposed to the general reader, perhaps he should have omitted such Songs entirely.

Of more interest are poems in praise of friends who were literary figures—of Ezra Pound and of William Carlos Williams, for example. The Song to Pound on his eightieth birthday, in 1965, is more moving than Berryman's prose "Tribute" to that poet, primarily because it does not express any of the reservations that the prose work contains ("I cannot consider him the peer of Eliot as a poet," Berryman says there).[39] The Song concentrates rather on Pound's personal qualities—his love of tennis, his intellect, and his generous concern for other writers, as evinced by his constant efforts to encourage them and to aid them financially (224). Similarly, the Song to Williams emphasizes that man's friendliness to aspiring poets (324, "An Elegy for W. C. W., the lovely man").

We may notice in several of the Songs to friends who were also poets a tendency of Henry's *not* to praise their literary achievements, or at least to have reservations about them. Henry seldom seems to be able to forget that these men are, after all, his competitors. The Songs to Delmore Schwartz mention more than once. that his work declined in quality after the early years (150,157). The Song to Louis MacNeice is self-serving; when MacNeice was making a documentary film in 1953 about the conquest of Mount Everest, Henry says that he had to inform him of Leigh-Mallory's answer to the question of why a man chooses to climb a mountain—" 'because it is there' " (267). In fairness, we must note that Henry does not make such comments about all his friend-poets; he does add that MacNeice wrote well, and he does not mention any weaknesses in Randall Jarrell's work or his mind. Jarrell is said to have written many books, all of high quality (121).

In Henry's expressions of love he has progressed beyond the Berryman of the *Sonnets* and *Homage,* who had difficulty distinguing between that emotion and lust. There are several declarations of love for his third wife, Kate, and for his children. Dream Song 171 begins by modifying Pound's "Envoi," itself an echo of Edmund Waller's "Go, Lovely Rose":

> Go, ill-sped book, and whisper to her . . .
> that she is beautiful. . . .
>
> Say her small figure is heavenly & full. . . .
> Say she is soft in speech, stately in walking,
> modest at gatherings, and in every thing
> declare her excellence.
>
> Forget not, when the rest is wholly done
> and all her splendours opened one by one
> to add that she likes Henry,
> for reasons unknown, and fate has bound them fast
> one to another in linkages that last
> and that are fair to see.

This love poem seems to me more satisfactory than the earlier "Canto Amor" because here the love and the joy are implicit rather than insistently proclaimed. The joy of love for both wife and daughter, "Twissy," is included in a later Song that indicates that Henry has found a large degree of contentment in his domestic life (186). "Twissy," Henry's "almost perfect child" (298), is praised along with Paul, Henry's son by his second wife, in Song 303, a poem that concludes with Henry's assertion that having a vocation, children, and friends is the real purpose in life.

Despite Henry's domestic happiness, he is incorrigible in lusting after beautiful women. He recalls Lise and that summer years ago (108, 183), two girls he had known in London during the 1930's (371), and a nude lady bending over a telephone, her "white rear bare in the air" (93). He dreams of the innumerable girls in the world, longing to seduce them all (350), and manages to meet many of them—a "Miss Birnbaum" (227); an "Yvette Choinais" (289, 332, 350); an unnamed hostess who entices him (142); a "Mrs Boogry" whom he admits he does not love but still slavers over (69); the daughter of a famous woman, unspecified, whom he seduced beside a swimming pool in Utah (343); and many others. Fortunately, the tone of most of these recollections differs from the unadulterated passion of the *Sonnets*. Characteristic is Henry's response when he sees a stranger in a restaurant:

> Filling her compact & delicious body
> with chicken páprika, she glanced at me. . . .
> and only the fact of her husband & four other people
> kept me from springing on her
>
> or falling at her little feet and crying
> 'You are the hottest one for years of night
> Henry's dazed eyes
> have enjoyed, Brilliance. ' . . .
>
> —Black hair, complexion Latin, jewelled eyes
> downcast . . . The slob beside her   feasts . . . What wonders is
> she sitting on, over there?
>
> (4)

The tone is both humorous and lascivious, but the humor predominates. Henry is more of a dirty old (or middle-aged) man than he is an adulterer. He notes that his increasing age has made it somewhat easier to avoid lust; by a conscious effort, he makes "passes" at ladies only in his correspondence with them, not in the flesh (350).

More of Henry's expressions of friendship and love are noted when we discuss later the theme of loss. The poet's domestic happiness is a quality not present in the earlier verse and is in a way charming. But, as in the *Sonnets* or *Homage,* the protagonist inhabits an existential world where love, marriage, friendship, children, and small pleasures only alleviate the pain of life; for unpleasant emotions dominate *The Dream Songs.* The consolations are real, but are only consolations.

VI *Psychological Disorder*

Berryman's interest in Freudian psychology had been evinced in the early poetry. "Desire Is a World by Night" (*Short poems,* 48-49) had speculated about the meaning of dreams. "The Traveller" (*Short Poems,* 13) had transcribed a dream, as Sonnet 79 later did. "Whether There Is Sorrow in the Demons" (*Short Poems,* 82-83) connected nightmare with guilt. "A Winter-Piece to a Friend Away" (*Short Poems,* 87-88) dealt with the madness of the poet, a friend, and the German poet Hölderlin. "The Lightning" (*Short Poems,* 78) suggested the Freudian notion of the prevalence of neurosis in Western society—in that poem, Berryman, his sister-in-law, and her children were all undergoing psychoanalysis; and everyone else should be, the poem claimed. "Fare Well" (*Short Poems,* 15) had mentioned the poet's father, with whom he "fought for mother," and therefore repeated Freud's insistence on the conflict between fathers and sons.

Berryman's fascination with mental disorder was stimulated when he began to undergo psychoanalysis in 1947 and when he applied his semiprofessional knowledge of psychology in his study of Stephen Crane, especially in the fourth and fifth chapters of that work; and this interest continues in the Dream Songs. Henry is obsessed with the mental difficulties of himself and others, even when he can offer no explanation of them. One of the best Songs about Schwartz catalogues the madnesses of that poet's last years. According to Song 154, Schwartz was convinced that everyone was attacking him and that his friends had rejected him; he claimed that Dwight MacDonald had taken his house, that Saul Bellow had refused him a loan, and that Henry had not been willing to help him during a trying time in 1957 ("Henry was in Asia," the poem notes, just as Berryman was making his trip to India for the State Department). In 1962-63, when Berryman was teaching at Brown University, Schwartz journeyed from Cambridge, Massachusetts, to Providence, Rhode Island, to talk with Henry, although the purpose of the conversation was never clear. Later that night Schwartz telephoned from New York City and asked Berryman to bring his wife and daughter to come live in New York, offering to pay their expenses if they would do so.

Such Songs achieve an emotional force simply by the presentation of facts, much in the same way that psychological case histories can. Another example is Song 135, where Henry morbidly and desperately recites some of the unpleasant details about two mass slayings of 1966—the killing of eight nurses in Chicago by Richard Speck, and the murders of his wife, his mother, and twelve others by Charles Whitman, who had climbed the library tower at the University of Texas in Austin and proceeded to shoot in all directions with a high-powered rifle. Later, in Dream Song 145, Henry compares his father's madness to that of Whitman.

Berryman follows Freudian theory in insisting on the importance of dreams as embodiments of the unconscious drives and on the primacy of the sex drive. Several consciously Freudian dream-symbols occur in the Dream Songs. Henry says that as an adolescent he sometimes dreamed of flying (11); "flying is regularly a symbol of sexual activity in male dreams" (*Stephen Crane,* 317). When Henry's father had once taken him on military maneuvers, he had said, "My field-glasses surpass . . . yours" (241), restating the sexual competition between father and son. Henry mentions several times the extraction of his teeth, a symbol, Freud says, of "castration as a punishment for onanism."[40]

Berryman consciously echoes Freud in the various emotions he expresses toward his mother. He has said that he has enjoyed a "close" relationship to her,[41] and praises her for her "courage" (100), but elsewhere he sees her as "armed" and dangerous (212). In one surrealistic poem she attacks Henry and his brother, hurling balloons or sacks filled with water down on them from a café terrace. The reason for her assault is that Henry has failed to order for her a dessert with "a Catholic name" (317). Henry hallucinates in Song 270, as he accepts Freud's notion that all men desire to return to the womb; he then inexplicably tries to kill his mother.

At times, Henry denies Freudian psychology; he disagrees with Freud's emphasis on the Oedipal conflict, and more especially with the theories that the latent content of dreams is made up of the unconscious concerns of the infant or the small child and that the manifest, or apparent, content of dreams is taken from the recent activities of the dreamer. Henry claims to have carried one of his own dreams to "forty-three structures" of interpretation, and he feels that the period of youth is more important to the psyche than that of childhood or infancy because, in his case, the greatest trauma occurred when he was eleven, not earlier. Henry concludes that Freud has "enlightened" us but insists that he oversimplified; a dream is not made up simply of latent and manifest content but is a "panorama / of the whole mental life" that is far more complex than Freud imagined (327).

Many of the Dream Songs are dreams or nightmares transcribed without explanation — 129, 202, 322, 368 and others — but I am not qualified to interpret them or, in fact, to amplify Berryman's relationship to psychological theory. Henry's obsessive emotions, however, are sufficiently clear for us to categorize them. Simplified, they are loneliness, anxiety, guilt, and a desire for death that conflicts with a fear of it. Freud defines neurotic anxiety as fear "in regard to a danger we do not know"[42] and that best characterizes Henry's feelings about his recurring madness (17). The disorder is vague and indefinable but no less frightening and oppressive. Henry can sympathize with others who suffer from it, as he does when a troubled student asks in Song 242 to talk with him in his office. The girl asks him to close the door; then she begins to cry, and Henry cries in sympathy with her. But, when he asks her what the trouble is, she, like the older waiter in Hemingway's "Clean, Well-Lighted Place," can reply only, " 'Nothing. Nothing's the matter.' " Henry pities the girl and finds her situation to be like his. Henry needs such comforting more often than he gives it. He fights his madness (201), and sometimes can overcome it (17), but more often he is helpless before it (52).

One of Henry's recurring delusions is that he is under attack, as when he imagines himself being lynched (10, 236), or substitutes himself for the hounded criminal in *High Sierra,* the 1941

Humphrey Bogart-Ida Lupino movie (9). (Bogart played the part of Roy Earle, a man trapped by circumstances; after committing a robbery, he is pursued into the mountains, outflanked, and shot. The "folks" mentioned in the Song are from the movie, an old man and his crippled granddaughter who are victims of capitalism and whom Earle had helped in several ways.)

Once again Henry tries to withstand assaults upon himself in a humorous description of a defensive position, a scene that is out of science fiction. The attackers are never specified, but Henry knows that they are out there somewhere:

> I hummed a short blues. When the stars went out
> I studied my weapons system.
> Grenades, the portable rack, the yellow spout
> of the anthrax-ray: in order. Yes, and most
> of my pencils were sharp.

(50)

Despite his defenses, Henry knows that he cannot withstand the attack, for he is outnumbered and will eventually be overrun.

Such delusions of persecution are, Henry realizes, a concomitant of the guilt he often feels. In Song 20, he judges and finds himself wanting—he has left letters unanswered, has daydreamed while others were talking to him, has lied, and has "hurt" several people with his curtness; and now he doubts that he has ever done good for others. Henry agrees with a court that finds him to be "The Man Who Did Not Deliver," guilty not only of the stated charges but also of numerous "un-charges" (43). He sometimes imagines being punished by having his "hands" (81) or his "crotch" (8) taken away, or by having a phallic leg cut off by a surgeon (319); and he realizes that the tormentors are only doing what he himself feels to be fair—they are following his own admission of guilt (236).[43]

Curiously, Henry's awareness of his guilt does not always make him more tolerant of the weaknesses of others, particularly women. Christine Keeler, a principal in the Profumo scandal, and Lana Turner, whose boyfriend was knifed to death by her daughter, are self-righteously attacked (348). But what Henry most despises about these ladies is not their sexual activities so much as the use they made of the scandals in promoting their public careers as actresses. He is more tolerant toward Fatty Arbuckle, the silent-screen comedian who in 1921 was accused of the murder of Virginia Rappe (222). Arbuckle and the twenty-three-year-old actress were at a drunken party in Los Angeles and withdrew to a bedroom; Miss Rappe died four days later of peritonitis. Arbuckle was tried three times—the first two trials ended in hung juries; the third, in acquittal.

Henry's anxiety and guilt make his life almost unbearable. He asks heaven to convert him into a Prufrockian mullusk, to make him blind to the beauty of women and unresponsive to sexual impulse (25). The desire to escape the disorder of life is a death-wish; the image of a mollusk is repeated from the early poem "On the London Train," in which such simple sea creatures escape the needs and torments of man and the higher animals. Henry seems only too willing to be punished by death for his indiscretions and again imagines himself, as he had done in Sonnet 73, as one of Kafka's tormented souls: "Henry, monstrous bug, laid himself down / on the machine in the penal colony / without a single regret" (310). To place the man-sized "bug" on the infernal "machine" is a conscious confusion of Kafka's stories "Metamorphosis" and "In the Penal Colony"; the purpose is to express the self-denigration and guilt that were Kafka's persistent themes.

Suicide is a possible alternative to simply awaiting death, and Henry considers it many times. Once, he imagines himself to be dead (in the series of Songs entitled "Opus Posthumous"—78-91); and then, like Lazarus, he is brought back to life. He decides, however, that the grave is a finer and more private place than this life and goes back to it "with a shovel / digging like mad" (91), seeking to return. He speculates that it is time for him to give in to death (159), and considers poison or a gun (40) or defenestration (196) as methods; but he finally rejects suicide as a solution. "Vanish me later," he says (the verb here is both imperative and declarative, in a dialectical distortion of syntax and voice), and concludes that he will stay alive while others kill themselves (196).

Henry longs to die, but his impulse is never obeyed (259) for several reasons. In Song 345, the messiness, the shame of committing one more evil act, and the pain he would cause family and friends dissuade Henry from self-destruction; but more often, his fear of death turns him away from suicide. Berryman was inexact in saying that Henry's fear of death is not clear in *The Dreams Songs*,[44] for it is implicit in Henry's view of the finality of death and explicit in several Songs. As he watches a Memorial Day parade, Henry recounts "the panic dread" he feels every morning when he wakes up, the anxiety and pain of life; but, as he remembers the purpose of the celebration — to celebrate the dead — he recalls his own cowardice (268): a fear of death that is greater than that of life. He jokingly decides that life "is not so bad, considering / the alternative . . ." (288). Henry is a "surviving Henry" (75) despite his longing for death;[45] he chooses to live.

Again we must be careful not to oversimplify, for Henry's feelings about life and death can easily be distorted by arranging certain Songs in an order that emphasizes one attitude or another. The Songs themselves are not arranged to indicate whether Henry basically loves life or detests it, for Henry's mixed attitudes toward both life and death are a turn of mind that Berryman had exhibited even in the early poetry—the tendency toward ambivalence. One of the reasons for the complexity of *The Dream Songs* is that Henry so often experiences, as we have observed, simultaneous and opposite emotions toward one object—toward his mother, God, America, fame, death, life, and himself. Such ambivalence is not always baffling. Once, when he has asked his friend whether he is a good man or a bad, he gets the reply that perhaps he is both good and bad at once, "like most of we" (239). At other times Henry's views form an unparaphrasable paradox, as when he claims that his increasing age makes death look "better" and, at the same time, "more fearful & intolerable" (185).

Whether clear or confusing, Henry's ambivalence is a part of his psychological makeup. Ambivalence in itself is not a manifestation of psychological disorder; and, although Henry's desperate loneliness, anxiety, guilt, and fear tend to excessiveness, they are emotions shared to some extent by everyone. Henry's commonality more than his strangeness makes his an interesting life..

Although unpleasant emotions dominate *The Dream Songs,* there is a wide variety of emotional experience embodied in these poems. Henry at times may suffer from nightmares, but he is also subject to insomnia. Song 326 humorously describes a Henry who tries virtually every sleeping position without success; he comforts himself with the thought that at least the terrors of his dream life cannot bother him as long as he lies awake. The poem concludes ambiguously with Henry's trying to decide whether a life of insomnia is better or worse than being dead. Other Songs reveal a breadth of emotional experience. Henry can be angry (336), or calm and appreciative of nature (62), or, as we have seen, anxious, lusty, guilty, self-pitying, religious, fatherly, despairing. Although he lives close to the nerve-ends, he can even claim to be bored, as he says he is in this Song, one of the most successful:

> Life, friends, is boring. We must not say so . . .
> and moreover my mother told me as a boy
> (repeatingly) 'Ever to confess you're bored
> means you have no
>
> Inner Resources.' I conclude now I have no
> inner resources, because I am heavy bored.
> Peoples bore me,
> literature bores me, especially great literature. . . .
>
> And the tranquil hills, & gin, look like a drag
> and somehow a dog
> has taken itself & its tail considerably away
> into mountains or sea or sky, leaving
> behind: me, wag.

(14)

The purported boredom here is belied by the ironic humor, the poem's basic emotion. But if any single feeling dominates *The Dream Songs,* it is the same sense of loss that had hovered over the early poems, the *Sonnets,* and *Homage.*

VII *Loss*

Berryman has said that Henry has suffered "an irreversible loss" (*Dream Songs,* vi); Henry uses the word "loss" itself several times without specifying what has been lost (73, 101, 168, 195). Sometimes he seems to suffer a generalized sense of dispossession, a feeling that things just have not worked out (1). Elsewhere, Henry is more specific. The "loss of friends" (276) through their departure recalls the early "Farewell to Miles" (*Short Poems,* 50-51). The "witchy ball" of Song 19 is a reference to the symbolic loss in "The Ball Poem" (*Short Poems,* 14). A loss of love similar to that suffered in the *Sonnets* informs at least two Dream Songs (5, 139). In Song 5, it is Henry's second wife rather than his first that he now rejects; in

139, the girl lost seems not to be Lise but one of the friends of Henry's youth. Henry bemoans his loss of the simplicity of childhood, wishing he could return to the cowboy movies and Saturday serials he had enjoyed back in Oklahoma. In Song 7, he remembers the heroic movie cowboys "Hoot" Gibson and William S. Hart; the scenes recalled are those of the simple melodramas that Berryman had longed for in "The Enemies of the Angels," "The Dispossessed," and *Homage*. Now that he is middle-aged, Henry is dejected also by the loss of his youth (263-64) and of the confidence he had enjoyed when he was twenty-two years old and "high on the hog" (65). Then, he was a young poet who loved life, he claims; but now he is a "wreck" (283).

Death is the major cause of loss in Henry's life. He recalls his grief for Bhain Campbell (88), his friend who had died in 1940. He grieves the passing of many of the great literary figures of our age—Yeats, Thomas, Hemingway, Frost, Faulkner, Williams, Stevens (36)—and becomes more morose as members of his own generation die—Theodore Roethke, Randall Jarrell, Delmore Schwartz (153). His friends Schwartz and Jarrell are mourned more often than any others—the former in a series of twelve elegiac and sometimes bathetic Songs (146-57), the latter in Songs 90, 121, and 127. William J. Martz tells us that Berryman, on his return from Cambridge, had first met Schwartz in New York in 1938. The two became close friends, and remained so while they were teaching at Harvard in the early 1940's[46] and until Schwartz's death in 1966. Berryman had known Randall Jarrell since 1939. Jarrell's poems entitled "The Rage for the Lost Penny" (a title that in its implications of youth and loss would appeal to Berryman) were collected alongside Berryman's in *Five Young American Poets* (1940), and the two poets had only respect for each other's work. Jarrell had reviewed *The Dispossessed* favorably, despite his tendency toward acerbity—a habit of being "Honest & cruel" as Berryman puts it (121).[47] Although Jarrell is not named in Song 127, it is he whose death was judged to be a suicide; in 1965, he had stepped in front of a car on a lonely road in North Carolina.

The death of writers and friends by suicide is a topic Henry cannot avoid. As we have noted, Henry is obsessed with suicide, his own and others'. He refers to others besides Jarrell—for example, to Thomas Chatterton (263); to Heinrich von Kleist ([310] a German dramatic poet who killed himself in 1811); and to Sylvia Plath

(153), the brilliant young American poet who married Ted Hughes and had two children, but who never overcame the death of her father (he had died of illness when she was a child) and who took her own life in 1963. In Henry's words, she is "one more suicide" to add to the others he broods over (172).

Ernest Hemingway, who killed himself with a shotgun in 1961, is mourned in Song 235 and is the unnamed suicide of Song 34:

> My mother has your shotgun. One man, wide
> in the mind, and tendoned like a grizzly, pried
> to his trigger-digit, pal. . . .
>
> Now—tell me, my love, *if* you recall
> the dove light after dawn at the island and all. . . .
>
> Why should I tell a truth? when in the crack
> of the dooming & emptying news I did hold back—
> in the taxi too, sick—
> silent—it's so I broke down here, in his mind
> whose sire as mine one same way. . . .

The Song is not ultimately clear, but elements of it are. Henry finds a crucial similarity between himself and Hemingway—the father of each man had committed suicide, shooting himself with a pistol ("whose sire as mine one same way"). Hemingway's mother, strangely and horribly, sent the suicide gun to her son, at his own request.[48] The clause "My mother has your shotgun" recalls that act and suggests that Henry's mother, simply by having the gun, wants him also to commit suicide; or, since she has not sent it to him, she does *not* want him to. The ambiguity purposefully repeats Henry's mixed feelings about his mother and about his own possible suicide. The phrase "the dove light after dawn at the island" does not refer to Hemingway's death but to the suicide of Henry's father, as we shall see in an examination of the images Henry associates with that death. The reference to being sick in a taxi seems to refer to another death entirely, for Henry was not in a taxi when he learned of his father's death; and in Song 235, he shed "tears in a diningroom in Indiana" for Hemingway. Whoever it was who was mourned in the taxi is associated both with Hemingway and with Henry's father ("a cab" is mentioned in Song 42, a poem about Henry's father's death) because he too must have been a suicide.[49]

The suicide of Henry's father occupies his mind more than any other; that is the death about which Henry is "an expert" (136). Some of the references to Henry's father are carefully veiled, as in Songs 6, 15 (the father is the man who "hides in the land"), and 42; but generally in the Dream Songs, for the first time in his career, Berryman was able to discuss the circumstances in some detail. Song 143 mentions the death weapon and the father's threats, frightening both to John and his mother, to take his son with him on a final swim in the Gulf of Mexico. The threat to take Henry (or Henry's brother) on a swim to death is repeated in Song 145, where we learn also that the suicide occurred at daybreak during the summer and just outside Henry's window. The place, the time of day, and the location of the wound are specified in Song 384: the father "shot his heart out in a Florida dawn" (with a dual meaning for "heart"). The specific locale of the island is mentioned in Songs 34 and 76; it is the same mysterious island that recurs in Henry's dreams (25). Both John Allyn Smith's death certificate and an article about the suicide in the Tampa *Sunday Tribune* (June 27, 1926, 5-A) identify the locale as Clearwater Island. That article also describes the position of Smith's body as "spread eagle," a phrase that Berryman repeats in Song 76. He either read that article or is recalling what he saw as a boy; in either case, he is being painfully explicit.

Henry's father was buried in Oklahoma, alongside a brother named Will (143). The image of a father who "will not swim back / ruined in a grave in Oklahoma" (292) is not so surrealistic as it seems; the reference is to the father's threat to swim to his death, the threat he fulfilled in effect by shooting himself.

The emotions that Henry expresses toward his father are, as we would expect, ambivalent. Thrice he explicitly states his continuing love for his father (143, 145). But rage and despair dominate the last reference to the father, in the penultimate Dream Song. Henry stands before his father's grave, longing not to be darkly moved by the thought of his father's suicide. Unable to feel indifference, he spits on the grave; and he ends the poem in a vicious and mad wish to re-kill his father:

> I'd like to scrabble till I got right down
> away down under the grass

and ax the casket open ha to see
just how he's taking it, which he sought so hard . . .
                                              & then Henry
will heft the ax once more, his final card,
and fell it on the start.

                                                              (384)

Henry's presence at the gravesite is only an imagined scene if
William J. Martz is correct in saying that Berryman never returned
to it.[50] The angry wish to kill the father is a result of the emotions
that Henry has suffered because of his father's death—fear, angst
resentment, a sense of desertion. These are the emotions that
Berryman finds dominant in the first two of Stephen Crane's
"Sullivan County Sketches." Like Berryman, Crane was only a boy
when his father died. Berryman feels that the sketches are based
upon that loss and present a "world . . . of perfect aloneness, in
which relations are possible only through rage and fear" (37-40).
Henry's fear and aloneness are clear in other Dream Songs; his rage
is fully expressed in the scene of axing his already-dead father. That
Berryman had the "Sullivan County Sketches" in mind as he wrote
Song 384 is suggested by the phrase "his final card"; the first sketch
presents a mysterious old recluse who plays cards with a younger
man and "cleans the little man out and howls 'Go.'" ". . . We have
here," Berryman says, "a fantasy on Crane's father and the child's
sense of abandonment (impoverishment) as his resented death . . ."
(*Stephen Crane,* 39).[51]

The loss of identity that Berryman feared in the *Sonnets* and that
is implicit in *Homage* does not seem to me a loss that Henry suffers
in *The Dream Songs.* The protagonist here undergoes periods of
madness and anxiety, but it is as if Henry has accepted these
feelings as a necessary part of his fragmented personality. Henry
knows who he is; he understands himself and his complexities. That
Berryman had almost come to terms with his greatest loss, that of
his father, is suggested by the fact that, in the fifty-nine poems of
Love & Fame, his father is mentioned only thrice and then only
briefly. The writing of the Dream Songs may have been in itself a
form of therapy that allowed Berryman to confront and to partly
allay his deepest anxieties.

VIII   The Dream Songs: *Form, Style, Tone*

The stanzaic pattern of *The Dream Songs*—three six-line stanzas, variously rhymed—was foreshadowed by the early "Nervous Songs" (*Short Poems*, 68-76). In the same way that he modified Yeats's eight-line stanza for *Homage,* Berryman borrowed this pattern from Yeats,[52] probably from some of that poet's *Last Poems* (1936-39), one of the six books that Henry took with him on his trip to Ireland (312, 279). But, Berryman adds, Yeats's "songs don't really resemble mine. . . . [The Dream Song form] is rather like an extended, three-part sonnet."[53] Berryman felt that the eighteen-line form allowed him more working room than the sonnet form.

The basic metrical pattern of the Dream Song stanza is 5,5,3,5,5,-3, but there are frequent variations. The rhyme pattern is more like that of three sestets than an extended sonnet, with variations like those of Petrarchan sestets. Berryman's patterns for single stanzas are often *aabccb, abcabc,* or *abcbac,* schemes in which the trimeter lines (3 and 6) rhyme. Some of the other patterns are *aaabbb, abacbc, abbacc.* Sometimes rhyme increases in frequency within a Song. In Song 337 there are no rhyming lines in the first stanza, four in the second, six in the last. Berryman occasionally chooses to ignore rhyme entirely.

Although the Songs consistently return to these patterns of meter and rhyme, very few of them—perhaps none of them—follow the basic form exactly. One that almost does is Song 285 (a poem that remains opaque even after the difficult words are defined). From its line 7, it reads:

> weathering Henry kept on his own side,
> whatever in the name of God that side was.
> And he struggled, pal.
> Apricate never: too he took in his stride
> more than most monsters can. Whatever the cause
> they called him Madrigal
>
> and Introit, passing him on the road
> wherever they were going and were gone.
> Henry peered quite alone
> as if the worlds would answer to a code
> just around the corner, down gelid dawn,
> beckoning like a moan.

The rhyme pattern is *abcabc, defdef, ghighi;* the meter is the standard 5,5,3,5,5,3, with the exception of line 9, which must be read, awkwardly, as a beheaded line if it is to have three feet. More likely it is a dimeter line, an anapest and an iamb. All the other lines can be analyzed according to the standard accentual-syllabic metrical practice of poetry in English, but some of them show a greater variety than is usual. Line 8, if I read it correctly, is an example: "whătévĕr / iñ thĕ / náme ŏf / Gód thát / sĭde wás." The line begins with an amphibrach—unusual in itself—has a pyrrhic, a trochee, and concludes with two spondaic feet. The trochee is the only base foot in the line. Elsewhere in the poem Berryman seems attracted to the falling rhythm of trochaic or dactylic feet. Lines 5 and 17 begin with three trochaic feet; lines 4, 7, 10, 11, 15, and 18 all begin with a trochee, line 8 with a dactyl. This tendency Berryman may have learned from Pound, who felt that falling rhythm was more natural to our language than the standard iambic pattern; Berryman has said that the "basal rhythm [he hears in Pound's *Cantos*] is dactylic,"[54] a falling rhythm. The basic rhythm of the Dream Songs seems to be iambic, but with many variations into falling rhythm.

As was true in *Homage,* the pattern of meter and rhyme often leads to making each stanza a unit; certainly each Song, with few exceptions, is a significant unit. This tendency has both good and bad results. On the one hand, the reader is not confronted with long sections of poetry which must be read consecutively in order to be understood; on the other, some of the poems have a conclusion that is too abrupt, an effect that is difficult to avoid when a poem concludes with a short line. Examples are "Thank you for everything" (25), "If I had to do the whole thing over again / I wouldn't" (28), or the conclusion of one of the elegies for Delmore Schwartz that recalls other poets dead: Song 146 expresses Henry's despair and anger as he insists that he has tried to become one with his dead compatriots but is now tired of doing so, for he is as undeniably alive as they are dead. The last line of the poem is unprepared for, and is too flip: "which brings me to the end of this song." English teachers will be reminded of student papers in which the writer's inability to bring his thoughts to a conclusion results in an abrupt and irrelevant closing sentence.

Berryman's experiments with rhyme are carried in *The Dream*

Songs to new heights—or have sunk to new depths, depending on the reader's views about the limits of rhyme. Our century has seen a revolution in the techniques of rhyme, and Berryman is one of the insurgents. "Often," he says, the Dream Song stanza "has no rhyme at all, but it sounds as if it rhymed."[55] He uses many slant rhymes ("wounds-sounds" [120], "passage-message" [116]), assonantal or false rhymes ("roof-soon" [112], "cabin-habit" [218], "jerk-Grrrrrr" [336]), mixtures of masculine and feminine rhymes ("me-Henry" [334], "Kentucky-luck" [65]). The ear of all but the most convervative of readers is probably attuned to these kinds of rhyme; it has been half a century since Yeats began to prepare us for such variations. But Berryman carries his experiments further with rhymes such as "languages-ages" (208), "indignities-promise" (100), "palfrey-valley" (315), "wholly-Henry" (380). Readers who agree with Karl Shapiro that "blink-brisk" can be considered a kind of slant rhyme[56] probably can accept any of Berryman's experiments as satisfactory or even pleasing; those who agree with Robert Hillyer that slant rhyme itself is suspect[57] will be irritated by Berryman's variations.

Such unusual rhymes contribute to the original style of *The Dream Songs.* As we have noted, the unity of the volume is not simply "in the style alone,"[58] as one reviewer insists; but its style is one of its great accomplishments. In the Songs, "we actually hear a style creating itself," as Berryman said of Henry Reed's "Lessons of the War."[59] The style of *The Dream Songs* is not, however, entirely an innovation for Berryman; he had perfected many of the stylistic devices as early as the *Sonnets* or *Homage:* literary, historical, or personal allusions; clichés and altered clichés; puns; neologisms and changes in parts of speech; ellipses; syntactical inversions; and finally, a wide variety in levels and kinds of diction—foreign, archaic, formal, dialectical, colloquial, baby-talk, slangy, vulgar. Dream Song 48 furnishes many examples:

> He yelled at me in Greek,
> my God!—It's not his language
> and I'm no good at—his is Aramaic,
> was—I am a monoglot of English
> (American version) and . . . pieces from
> a baker's dozen others. . . .

> The seed goes down, god dies,
> a rising happens,
> some crust, and then occurs an eating. He said so,
> a Greek idea,
> troublesome to imaginary Jews, . . .
>
>
> Cawdor-uneasy, . . . mourning
> the whole implausible necessary thing.
> He . . . sybilled of
> the death of the death of love.

The Song begins with an echo of "Christ's wild cry to God from the cross (Mark 15),"[60] "My God . . . why has thou forsaken me?" Henry's exclamation of "my God" is both a slangy expression of surprise and also an indication that he too feels abandoned by God. The Song has other typical stylistic elements: the ellipsis in the third line; the cliché "a baker's dozen"; the puns on "rising" and "some crust"; the allusions to *Macbeth* and to Berryman's story "The Imaginary Jew"; the conversion of the noun "sibyl" into the verb "sybilled"; the slangy "pal"; the periphrasis of "the death of the death of love."

One quality the Song does not have is incomprehensibility. It poses some difficulties—the "He" of line 16 could be either the god who yelled in line 1 or Henry himself, who, we remember, views poetry as a kind of priesthood. But, like most of the Dream Songs, this one is sufficiently clear. It concerns Henry's reservations about but final acceptance of the miracle of the Eucharist—however "implausible" it is, it is still "necessary."

Other stylistic elements that developed from the earlier Berryman are the nervous energy that infuses this and most of the Dream Songs, and the use of various pronouns to designate one personality—again, as in "The Ball Poem," with the purpose of allowing the poet to both reveal and conceal himself. Stylistic elements of the Song that seem to me progressions beyond the earlier Berryman are the more expressly colloquial voice of the poem (it is meant to be spoken, it *is* spoken to us if read aright) and the improvisational effect achieved by the correction of the verb "is" to "was" in line 4 and by the afterthought "American version" enclosed in parentheses. The early poems, the *Sonnets,* and *Homage* never suggest such off-handedness; if anything, they seem too carefully worked.

This improvisational quality is of course a conscious effect. Again, Berryman is seldom a poet who allows his materials to be slack. The use of clichés—and there are many—is also thoroughly intended. It is likely that Berryman wants us to recall the original metaphors embedded in most clichés—in "lowered the boom," "a baker's dozen," and so on. Such expressions were once original and effective; to find them used consciously may remind us to seek out that originally powerful and specific meaning. Or the clichés may be used to contribute to the improvisational effect and to the collo- quial voice of the Dream Songs, since clichés readily are a function of the spoken language.

The Dream Songs have no single tone. Sufficient numbers of them have been quoted to indicate that the tone ranges widely through the levels of human emotion. William Meredith has written that the Dream Songs, taken together, are "essentially humorous,"[61] but the humor of the Songs is overlaid with Henry's unpleasant emotions—fear, loneliness, or anxiety. If read through in their entirety, the Songs are seriocomic in tone, similar to the Black Humor of Theater of the Absurd drama, similar to Samuel Beckett's *Waiting for Godot* or *Endgame*. The humor is a response to an existential world in which all man's activities, beliefs, attitudes are equally absurd. The humor is not an assertion that life is essen- tially a meaningful or pleasant occupation, for sadness is its source.

In his discussion of Stephen Crane's use of irony, Berryman has analyzed a seriocomic tone similar to that of *The Dream Songs*. He writes,

. . . Early Greek comedy presented a contest between the *Alazon* (Im- postor) and the *Eiron* or Ironical Man: after vauntings and pretensions, the *Alazon* is routed by the man who affects to be a fool. The Imposter pretends to be more than he is, the Ironist pretends to be less. Now in most of the criticism of Stephen Crane that displays any sensitivity, whether out- raged or not, one nearly makes out a nervous understanding that this author is simultaneously *at war with* the people he creates and *on their side*—and displays each of these attitudes so forcibly that the reader feels he is himself being made a fool of. . . . I wonder whether explanation will ease this feeling; for the truth is that, in a special and definite sense, the reader *is* being made a fool of. Who are the creations Crane is most at war with? His complex ones, his "heroes"? or his simplest ones, his babies, horses, dogs,

and brooks? With the first class his art is a Greek comedy, a contest with
the imposter. . . . So far as his creations of the first class are striving to
become members of the second class, they become candidates for pathos or
tragedy; so far as they fail, they remain figures of (this deadly-in-earnest)
comedy. . . .

There is regularly an element of pathos, therefore, in his ironic (op-
positional) inspection, and an element of irony regularly in his pathos. A
Crane creation, or character, normally is *pretentious* and *scared*—the
human condition; fitted by the second for pathos, by the first for irony.

(*Stephen Crane,* 278-80)

Several phrases here characterize the tone of *The Dream Songs:* the
writer is "simultaneously *at war with* the people he creates and *on
their side,*" a doubleness of view that makes the reader feel he is
"being made a fool of"; the writer and the reader contain both the
Imposter and the Ironical Man; the work becomes a mixture of
pathos and irony, tragedy and "deadly-in-earnest" comedy.

The writer's tone in such a work becomes intentionally mixed,
confused, ambiguous:

> There sat down, once, a thing on Henry's heart
> só heavy, if he had a hundred years
> & more, & weeping, sleepless, in all them time
> Henry could not make good.
> Starts again always in Henry's ears
> the little cough somewhere, an odour, a chime. . . .
>
> But never did Henry, as he thought he did,
> end anyone and hacks her body up
> and hide the pieces, where they may be found.
> He knows: he went over everyone, & nobody's missing.
> Often he reckons, in the dawn, them up.
> Nobody is ever missing.

(29)

The Song is about Henry's response to the death of the father, the
funeral itself (the "cough," "odour," and "chime"), and Henry's
hallucinations about killing others. Berryman quoted the poem in
1965 to illustrate his technique, and then he commented about it:
"Whether the diction of that is consistent with blackface talk, heel-
spinning puns, coarse jokes, whether the end of it is funny or
frightening, or both, I put up to the listener. Neither of the

American poets who as reviewers have quoted it admiringly has committed himself; so I won't."[62]

The form, the style, and the tone of the Dream Songs are undeniably original. Allen Tate has said that they "cannot be imitated,"[63] a judgment that the reviewer Philip Toynbee has tried to disprove by interspersing his own imitations of the Dream Song stanza among quotations from Berryman and by then inviting readers to guess which are his and which are the poet's.[64] Toynbee has missed Tate's point. Any distinctive style—Hemingway's, for example—can be imitated or parodied with some ease; but any such derivation will always be recognized as being in the style of the writer who first developed it, not the imitator's. Berryman made a style his own, and no one can imitate it without the source becoming immediately apparent. Unfortunately, the Dream Song style is as seductive as Hemingway's, and no doubt it will be echoed by other poets who hope to capture Berryman's originality and verve by copying his mannerisms. Berryman himself was aware of the danger of self-parody; and he strove in his last volumes, *Love & Fame* and *Delusions, etc.,* to develop a style that would not be imitative of the Dream Songs.[65]

CHAPTER 5

The Last Works

BERRYMAN'S reputation as an important poet was established with *The Dream Songs* but was not enhanced by *Love and Fame* (1970) or by the posthumously published *Delusions, etc.* (1972). What is most noticeable about these 102 unremarkable poems is that they were produced so soon after *The Dream Songs.*[1] Furthermore, Berryman's respectable reputation as a writer of fiction was harmed by the publication in 1973 of *Recovery,* an uncompleted novel. Even if Berryman had lived to polish the manuscript, *Recovery* seems to be unsalvageable as a work of art.

I Love & Fame: *Structure, Tone, Form, and Style*

Some readers may prefer *Love & Fame* to *The Dream Songs,* for these later poems are clearer, simpler, more direct. Virtually all the allusions, personal and literary, are either self-explanatory or are understandable if we have a knowledge of Berryman's life and his earlier poetry. An example is the thunderstorm that frightened Berryman's sister-in-law (*Love & Fame,* 87), an echo from the early poem here often leads directly into the next, a Yeatsian method of literary heroes are seldom new—"Mark" Van Doren (19, 28), "Cal" (Robert Lowell), "Saul" Bellow, "Elizabeth" Bishop, William "Meredith," "Bhain Campbell," "Randall" Jarrell (58), T. S. Eliot, James Joyce, William Butler Yeats (25), and so on.

Love & Fame is also more coherent than *The Dream Songs.* A Poem here often leads directly into the next, a Yeatsian method of organization seldom found in *The Dream Songs.* And each of the four sections of *Love & Fame* demonstrates a separate coherence based upon setting or theme. The first two sections are narratives. Part One is set at Columbia during Berryman's years there (1932-

36); Part Two recalls Berryman's stay at Cambridge (1936-38). Part Three, set in the year or two immediately preceding the publication of *Love & Fame*, is an account of obsessions and anxieties that drive the poet to a mental hospital. The section concludes with his returning home and bringing the manuscript of *Love & Fame* with him. Part Four, "Eleven Addresses to the Lord," is a calm, moving hymn of faith, a coda to the whole volume. Finally, as we shall see in a moment, all four sections are connected by variations on the themes that have consistently appeared in Berryman's work — sociopolitical concerns, the nature of art and poetry, religion, friendship and love, psychological disorder, and a sense of loss. In *Love & Fame*, these themes tend to cluster around the words of the title and to become more clearly interrelated than in the earlier works.

Despite its clarity and coherence, *Love & Fame* must suffer by comparison with *The Dream Songs*. The Songs found an almost perfect combination of tone, form, style, and content—a union that *Love & Fame* does not enjoy (182).

Generally, the tone of *Love & Fame* is calmer, quieter than that of *The Dream Songs*. The dominant emotions are serious, but not finally unpleasant. There is less humor here, although there is also less of the dark anxiety that overlaid *The Dream Songs*. Despite a reviewer's comment that *Love & Fame* has "enormous emotional range,"[2] the volume is more limited than *The Dream Songs* in the kinds and intensity of its emotions.

The form of most of the poems in *Love & Fame* is the quatrain, normally unrhymed and without a basic metrical pattern. Two of the poems—"Death Ballad" and "The Home Ballad"—are based on the ballad stanza; but Berryman has seemingly chosen elsewhere in these poems to forget his experiments with standard metrical practice and to follow his impulses. The rhythms of the poems are irregular, sometimes returning to a familiar pentameter line but usually free and loose.[3] The four-line stanza here is not really a form at all in any traditional sense. The Dream Song stanza had achieved the nearly impossible task of balancing innovation and tradition; *Love & Fame* tilts more toward innovation. Readers who feel that meter and rhyme are likely to remain in the center of the poetic tradition can be delighted by the Dream Song stanza, but they may conclude that *Love & Fame* has left the mainstream. We should not assume, however, that *Love & Fame* is careless in technique. Robert Lowell has commented that, "if Berryman's later work seems idiosyncratic, one should remember that he had the humility and stamina to pass all the hardest standard tests."[4] If Berryman writes in a form that approaches free verse, it must be because he chose to, not because his technical resources were limited.

Approaching Ireland and the future, Henry told us in *The Dream Songs* that he would not return with the same form and manner (Song 379). The style of *Love & Fame* is not totally distinct from that of *The Dream Songs;* the familiar Berryman devices are here—the colloquial voice, the mixed levels of diction, the experimentation with parts of speech, the inversions, the conscious clichés. Negro dialect is absent, for Berryman almost always speaks to us in the first person, without masks. These poems show fewer varieties of style than had *The Dream Songs.*

Perhaps Berryman was afraid of becoming a self-parodist if he continued to write Dream Songs, but the masochistic or self-congratulatory revelations in *Love & Fame,* spoken in the first person, often lack the aesthetic distance that Berryman had maintained behind the mask of Henry. For example, Henry mentions that he has three children (Dream Song 303), and we assume only that he has made another intended error with numbers. In *Love & Fame,* Berryman himself admits that he in fact did, by 1970, have three children, one of them illegitimate ("Her & It," 3); and the information is discomfiting to the reader, as other examples indicate. In "The Damned," the poet recalls an adulterous relationship. The woman speaks the first stanza of the poem, explaining that she is pregnant and suffers from considerable anxiety. The poet then describes the scene:

> As soon as I tucked it in she burst into tears.
> She had a small mustache but was otherwise gifted,
> riding, & crying her heart out.
>
> (She had been married two years) I was amazed;
> (Her first adultery) I was scared & guilty.
> I said 'What are you crying for, darling? *Don't.'* . . .
>
> She came again & again, twice ejecting me
> over her heaving. I turned my head aside

> to avoid her goddamned tears,
> getting in my beard.

(Love & Fame, 68)

There is nothing in this poem to indicate that the scene is an hallucination or a nightmare; if it recalls actuality, as it seems to do, the poem is unpleasantly revealing. Another example is "In & Out" (24), also a first person poem. It quotes a letter that Henry had written to the poet Robert Creeley, a letter that had agreed with a newspaper review of Creeley's work (probably the volume *For Love: Poems 1950-1960*) which called the poems " 'crushingly dull.' " Henry (and Berryman) adds that he did not need to read all the poems to arrive at his judgment that they, and Creeley, are "trivial." The letter concludes imperiously: "Pray do not write to me again. Pitch defilith. / Yours faithfully. . . ." Another blatant recollection occurs in "To B— E—" (52), where he describes a meeting with his lover from Cambridge, a meeting that took place in New York City some time after their first affair. The girl had undressed, "opened" herself, and said " 'Kiss me.' " One final example is Berryman's toting up his sexual conquests—the total was seventy-nine—and ranking the ladies according to their ability ("Thank You, Christine," 48). In his favor, Berryman had second thoughts about six of the weakest poems in *Love & Fame* and excluded them from a second edition in 1972.

There still remain, however, far too many passages in *Love & Fame* that suffer from the weakness of much of the confessional poetry of our time: the descent into embarrassing self-revelation. Berryman's purpose, like that of a fellow poet he mentions in "Cadenza on Garnette" (4), is to be completely frank. He quotes Wordsworth—" 'If I had said out passions as they were, / . . . the poems could never have been published' "—and then he says out the passions as they were. He has entirely mastered the reticence about himself that obscured some early poems and that led him to assume the mask of Henry; but there are some things we do not want to know about others, even if their motive in such confessions is honesty and forthrightness.

II Love & Fame: *Parts One and Two*

The first two sections of *Love & Fame* are consecutive narratives

that can be read together as an autobiographical remin-
iscence—despite Berryman's disclaimer that he is "not writing an
autobiography-in-verse" ("Message," 57). The themes of these two
parts are Berryman's youthful loves and his veneration of poets and
of recognition—love and fame. The dominant emotion of Parts
One and Two is not truly love but lust. The young man fondly
recalls moments when he and a coed sat in a guest parlor of a Barnard dormitory and engaged in sexual foreplay in plain sight of
anyone who passed the doorless room ("Cadenza on Garnette," 4).
He recites another instance of his lust in "My Special Fate" (12),
when he and a girl named "Clare Reese" left a Barnard dance and
took the subway to some park, probably near the upper tip of
Manhattan, where they undressed and enjoyed each other—at least
until they were sighted by some teenagers who laughed raucously as
the two hastily fumbled back into their clothes. In "Freshman
Blues" (9), he brags about his conquest of a "townie," not a coed,
whom he crawled into bed with while the girl's mother, cowed by
the young man's status, listened downstairs. (Apparently the girl's
brother was less impressed with the visitor's social position; the
poet says that he so feared the brother that he eventually turned the
girl over to another undergraduate.)

At least once his lust was frustrated when a girl named "Elspeth"
proudly told him that she had allowed someone to take
photographs of her in the nude and then she teasingly refused to let
the poet see the pictures ("Images of Elspeth," 10-11). But more
often than not his lust finds an outlet. After he had arrived at Cambridge the young man met a girl named "Christine" in a tearoom
and she immediately accompanied him to his rooms where she
suggested that perhaps they should wait a few days since she was
undergoing her period. The young man was not deterred, and the
girl is now praised for doing her "best" for him ("Thank You,
Christine," 48).

Throughout these scenes the young man is shown to have been
able to experience lust without necessarily feeling love, but he was
never able to express love without confusing it with lust—he lusted
after most girls and loved only a few; but, even when he expressed
love, it was always accompanied by lust. The confusion occurs in the
first two lines of *Love & Fame*—"I fell in love with a girl. / O and a
gash" ("Her & It," 3). And the same confusion is present at the
end of Part Two of *Love & Fame*. The last four poems of this sec-

tion express the culminating love of the young poet for a girl known to us only by her initials, "B. E.," perhaps an indication that the poet feels that this love affair was more nearly sacred for him than any of the other relationships with girls who are explicitly named. B. E. was a student at Newnham College, a former ballerina, and beautiful. The last of the poems to her, "To B— E—" (52) forms an ecstatic conclusion to the first half of *Love & Fame,* but even here the poet now admits that his love for the girl was confused with a "thirsting & burning lust." There is no affair in Parts One and Two that fails to reveal that for the young man love was always, finally, lust.

Fame was the other obsession of the young poet. He imagined the delight of someday having his name widely known and praised ("My Special Fate," 12). His great admiration for Auden (7), Yeats (19), Unamuno (21), Pound, Eliot, Joyce (25), and others seems to have been based as much on the fame they had achieved as on the inherent worth of their literary works. The young man conceived of himself as being, like his heroes, an exile by virtue of his profession; he compares himself, an American expatriate, with Matthew Arnold, who was speculating, alone, on Mount Etna while his contemporaries were entertaining themselves at the Great Exposition of 1851 ("Two Organs," 17). Finding such analogies between himself and his heroes, the young Berryman hoped also that their fame would become his.

Although he placed himself in the best of company, especially that of Yeats and Auden, the young poet was unsure of his stylistic direction; he realized that their styles could not become his, however much he admired them, and that his own style was not yet developed ("Two Organs," 16). Sometimes, when diligent revision failed to result in the exactly right word or phrase for a difficult line, the young man feared that he would never be a poet at all or feared even more an *"insignificance"* ("Friendless," 42), and he means not only that he wanted his poems to be filled with meaning but also that he hoped to become a writer of renown. His fears were infrequent; usually he is presented as having been as confident as he was when he replied to a coed's admiring comment that he was a poet by saying that he was not a very good one yet, "but probably would be" ("Tea," 50). Earlier, on the ship taking him to England, he apostrophized Yeats, said that he himself was on his way, actually and figuratively, and that Yeats's publishers would eventually have to bring out Berryman's own poetry. The young man admits that he has not fully mastered the secrets of his craft, but adds, "I swamp with possibility" ("Away," 35). This poem, like many others in *Love & Fame,* achieves a delightful humor and irony by presenting the younger Berryman through the eyes of the older one. The young man's confidence is now understood to have been as absolute as that of Stephen Dedalus, and as egotistical—an insight that escaped the young poet. Similar to the point of view of the *Sonnets,* this double view achieved by a man analyzing an earlier self is one of the pleasures of *Love & Fame.*

The young Berryman's hankering for fame is discovered to have been as excessive as his sexual appetite ("In & Out," 24), and the poet is as uncertain now as he was then as to which of the two was more important to him at the time. The girls seem to be more important in "Two Organs" (16-17) which begins with a longing for fame but concludes with a sexual fantasy. The poet quotes a fishing-companion, who longs to have an immense erection, one big enough to fill a lake. The poet admits to having a similar dream when he was at Columbia—to seduce at the same time all the coeds at Barnard and at Smith College, and then to proceed to the secretarial students at the Katherine Gibbs School. But in "Images of Elspeth" (10-11) poetry is recalled as having been more important than individual females. The girls are confused in the poet's mind, whereas his "Muse," although perhaps taking her origin from real girls, has always been a separate entity. In both "Two Organs" and "Images of Elspeth" real women and imaginative art are the dual goals the young man doggedly pursued, but he was confused, unable finally to decide which of the two ought to be more important. There was for him a conflict between physicality and art—the same conflict we have seen in the earlier poetry, notably in "The Animal Trainer" and in the *Sonnets.*

The young man of Parts One and Two betrays a lack of direction in other ways. Although alternately dedicated to girls and to poetry, he was once dazzled by the brilliance of a Richard Blackmur article in *Poetry,* ironically one that argued for the preëminence of poetry as a creative process capable both of describing and forming reality. As Berryman now recalls it in "Olympus" (18-19), he then read everything he could find by that critic and decided to become a critic himself. He admits that his girls, his classes, and his own poetry were neglected during the few weeks he devoted to literary criticism, a field he temporarily considered more profound and accurate than poetry. He prepared an analysis of Yeats's dramas, consciously employing Blackmur's diction and phraseology whenever possible. But this attraction to criticism was a temporary one; the young man's conflicting desires for love and for poetic fame were his recurring and dual goals; and they remain, throughout Parts One and Two of *Love & Fame,* an unresolved conflict of opposites.

III   Love & Fame: *Parts Three and Four*

Just as the first two sections of *Love & Fame* form a unit, so also do Parts Three and Four. The structure of these last two sections of the volume follows the archetypal pattern of death and rebirth, descent and ascent, loss and recovery. The first poem of Part Three, "The Search" (55-56) reveals the nature of the poet's loss to be religious. He compares himself to Einstein who, at the age of twelve, had lost his faith in God. Both the poet and Einstein responded to their loss of trust not with an intense desire to refute God, but to know Him; and they studied the writings of other men who had experienced similar doubts. Berryman was stimulated in his search by a nightmare he suffered while under anesthesia in a dentist's chair in Detroit, probably during his year there in 1939-40; he dreamed not only that he was himself dead, a fate that he could accept, but also that his poetry was being located, extracted, and destroyed by an omnipotent hand. His fear of the ultimate death of his works drove the poet to a spiritual quest through mythology and comparative religion and through the writings of Martin Luther, Lancelot Andrewes, and others.

The cause of this loss of faith is suggested in "The Search" by the reference to Einstein's age. Again, Berryman usually said that he too was twelve when his father shot himself and, although the poet had never explained the connection before, that death was the direct cause of his rejection of God. The sixth of the "Eleven Addresses to the Lord" (91) states the cause-effect relationship explicitly. There the poet says that it was his "father's suicide" that destroyed his "faith" and that he has experienced an awful loneliness since that time. The father's death and the resulting loss of belief are seen also in this poem as the sources of the "confusions & afflictions" that pursued the poet throughout his life and that form the subject matter of the first three Parts of *Love &*

Fame—lust, guilt, divorce, madness, despair, and a longing for fame.

After summarizing the initial loss of his father and his faith in "The Search," the poet begins in the subsequent poems of Part Three his descent into despair. The relationship of every poem in the section to that descent is not clear, but the second and third poems—"Message" (57) and "Relations" (58)—both refer to the many "losses" the poet has experienced, and we know that the losses are those of father, faith, wives, friends, youth, and confidence. (In "Relations," the word occurs as "*Losses*," because that is the title of one of Randall Jarrell's books of poetry, a volume published in 1948.)

The fourth poem of Part Three, "Antitheses," continues the poet's descent into confusion. It tries to puzzle out the ways of achieving fame. Some poets have been impractical and absent-minded; others, tough and realistic. Berryman concludes that no one can understand poets, not even the poets themselves; he does not speculate about which of the two kinds he is, or whether he is a combination of both. Instead, he turns to an objective description of his surroundings, as if by noting them he (and his readers) may somehow figure out the truth about the poet:

> My rocking-chair is dark blue, it's in one corner
> & swivels. . . .
> My wife's more expensive patchquilt rocker
> is five feet away & and does not swivel.
>
> (59)

In context, "Antitheses" is more than an expression of whimsical bewilderment about the nature of fame or of poets; the speaker here is at a loss in attempting to understand himself and is disturbed by his failure to do so.

The four poems that follow "Antitheses" are social and political. Since the poet cannot understand himself, he attempts to find orderliness in the outside world; but he is disappointed. "The Soviet Union" (60-61) criticizes Russian Communists for killing the writer Isaac Babel, who presumably died in a Russian labor camp in 1939 or 1940. Berryman does not totally condemn the Communists, as he had done in *The Dream Songs* and earlier; he admits that even Stalin had some noble characteristics. But still the world is a dark place, the Western hemisphere as well as the Eastern; the poem lashes America for intervening in Siberia in 1919 and for killing Martin Luther King, Indians, and others; and it sadly speculates that one of those killed may have been, like Babel, a man of genius.

The three additional sociopolitical poems — "The Minnesota 8 and the Letter-Writers," "Regents' Professor Berryman's Crack on Race," and "Have a Genuine American Horror-&-Mist on the Rocks"—are additional comments about the disorder of the contemporary American scene. The first (62) is the poet's response to a letter he has read in his newspaper, a complaint written from a hard-hat suburb of Minneapolis, St. Louis Park. The letter-writer wants the "Minnesota 8," a group of activists who were indicted for interfering with the Selective Service System, to be hanged for their actions. Berryman's liberalism shows as he calls the writer insane and reminds him that the signers of the Declaration of Independence similarly dared to break the law for a cause that was not popular at the time. He ironically notes that the man from St. Louis Park almost surely venerates those early American revolutionaries.

Although "The Minnesota 8 and the Letter-Writers" insists that "violence" is sometimes necessary to shock a complacent nation into comprehension, ". . . Berryman's Crack on Race" (63-64) angrily attacks black militants who preach war between the races, for Berryman's sympathy for Negroes seems to have reached its limit. Almost in despair, he agrees with Thomas Jefferson that the two races cannot live together in peace; and he irritatedly calls for the violent confrontation that the militants insist is necessary for social change. He points out that no rational people could want war, but that seems to be the likely outcome. He is especially angered by the sexual implications behind the demands of black militants. The solution he prefers is not total war between the races, but a union of the rational members of each race while the "fanatics," both black and white, "*have it out* & good riddance." However, he concludes that this solution is impractical. It is clear that, like Henry's wish to drop nuclear bombs on China, the poet's opinions here are born out of a sense of hopelessness in the face of insurmountable problems. "Have a Genuine American Horror-&-Mist on the Rocks" (65), the last of the sociopolitical poems, is a negligible squib, an occasional comment on the Army's plan to dump nerve-gas rockets into the Atlantic. The poem may be the first to use the word "ecology" and, I hope, the last; it has already become a cliché.

By their placement and their tone, these sociopolitical poems are associated with the poet's increasing despair, anxiety, and mental disorder in Part Three of *Love & Fame;* for he logically proceeds from disgust with the external world to unpleasant emotions that stem from within. "Damned" (68) is not only a description of an adulterous situation but also a presentation of the poet's guilt. He has been awake all night, despising himself; and the rising sun in the last line does not bring him absolution. "Of Suicide" recounts the familiar terror that Henry had experienced:

> REFLEXIONS on suicide, & on my father, possess me.
> I drink too much. My wife threatens separation.
> She won't 'nurse' me. She feels 'inadequate.'
> We don't mix together.
>
> (69)

The poet's anxiety is increasing here. "Dante's Tomb" (71) associates the death of that Italian poet, of Emily Dickinson, and of the Toltec culture of Mexico with Berryman's own demise. The poem disjointedly concludes with a recalled scene of lust: "She said to me, half-strangled, 'Do that again. / And then do the other thing.' " The association of lust with guilt, death, and disorder is familiar from the *Sonnets* and *The Dream Songs.*

Proceeding from his explanation of the boyhood beginnings of his descent, the references to his life-long difficulties, and his disgust at the current world-scene, the poet is again led into despair; and he calls one poem specifically by that title. "Despair" (72) is similar to the several Dream Songs which describe a mental disorder that is incapable of being catalogued or clearly explained, but the symptoms are explicit—an atmosphere of darkness, physical complaints, and nausea; a sense of ennui, exhaustion, and fragmentation.

Logically, the following poem, "The Hell Poem" (73-74), finds the poet in a mental hospital, lost in disorder and taking sedatives. The poem concludes with a nightmare he has suffered, a confused mixture of "witches," "a headless child," crying, terror, and separations. But the despair of this last scene in the poem is partly allayed by the earlier stanzas of "The Hell Poem," where the poet is more concerned about the other inmates than he is about himself.

He pities a young girl named "Tyson" who has been allowed to attend a wedding outside but was browbeaten by her mother until she returned to the hospital. He watches as others leave the ward to take shock treatments. And he is compassionate toward the hopeless cases, those dangerous to themselves or others, who are locked away in a separate part of the hospital. When one of these improves sufficiently to be allowed in the open ward, the poet and his friends are "ecstatic"; when one of them has to return to the locked ward, they are saddened.

Such compassion, not despair, is the dominant emotion in the following three poems, all of which have the hospital as their setting. Berryman's sympathy for the weak and the helpless is nowhere better expressed than in "Death Ballad" (75-76), perhaps because the poet himself had experienced the suffering he pities. The poem concerns Tyson and another nineteen-year-old girl, both of whom want only to die. The poet, who speculates sadly about the fate of the girls, concludes that no one can stop them from committing suicide if they choose to do so, and that no one can prevent their ultimate death even if they do not kill themselves. He urges them to love something outside themselves as an antidote to madness, and his own concern for the two girls is in itself a kind of therapy for him.

The poet makes his ascent to "Purgatory" (78-79) by expressing a similar compassion for a "Mrs Massey," an elderly widow who supervises the evening meal at the hospital. The poet, who has known the lady for years, renews the acquaintance during his recurring stays at the hospital. Habitually, she has made a point of coming to his table during the meal and asking him whether it was satisfactory. But one evening she adds, " 'It gives me honour to serve a man like you, / would you sometime write me out a verse or two & sign it?' " The poet is deeply moved by her usual concern and by her added request. He concludes this poem written about and for Mrs. Massey by comparing his situation to hers, by noting how successfully she manages to cope with life, and by finding strength in her expression of compassion and respect for him.

The following poem, "Heaven" (80), completes the poet's Dantean ascent. He here recalls another girl with whom he was in love, a girl who "forgave" him for the lust he once expressed to her. The girl had died in an automobile accident soon after she had married another man. The poet recalls her now not as a missed opportunity for a sexual conquest, as so many of the girls of his youth were remembered in Part One. Instead, he feels a sense of loss; he is able to realize that the lust he once felt for her was an ignoble expression of love.

Compassion and true love are not the only forms of love expressed in Part Three. In "Relations" (58) Berryman's declaration of friendship for Lowell and others is seen as a valid form of love—it has its "dividends"; but it is imperfect because it is mortal and therefore subject to loss. He recalls the death of Bhain Campbell; and, although he says that he has never tried to experience such a close friendship since then, he has been as deeply affected by the loss of more recent friends. The details of Randall Jarrell's suicide are sadly explained, even down to the telephone call that Jarrell had made to his wife immediately before his death—a call in which he discussed the future of their children. By its placement in Part Three, not long before the poet's descent, the friendship expressed in "Relations" is seen only as a consolation in life; it does not prevent despair. In the same way, the poet's love for his daughter Martha may alleviate despair but cannot forestall it ("Despair," 72).

Both friendship and compassion are proper expressions of love, but both are imperfect. They are reflections of the love of the Good, in Plato's sense; but the only perfect love is that for the ultimate Idea, which becomes God in Christian theology and in Part Four of *Love & Fame,* the "Eleven Addresses to the Lord." One reason for the power of these poems of faith is that Berryman, like Henry, refuses to say things he does not believe, regardless of religious orthodoxy. Like Henry, he tends to disbelieve in immortality either for the saved or the damned. The damned, he speculates, will simply fall into a dreamless sleep; and so also might those who were better sorts, "the more or less just." Perhaps such a final "Rest," a state of existence without awareness, is God's last and finest "gift" to man (Number 5 of "Eleven Addresses to the Lord"). And, again like Henry, the poet here is baffled by the problem of evil. In the second of the "Eleven Addresses," he credits God with all of creation, both good and evil: the beauty of spring and nature, the love of Christ for man, even the insights of Sigmund Freud are part of that creation and are considered to be saving graces that exist inexplicably alongside insanity, war, and other evils. (Again, World War II is the war that most captured Berryman's imagination; he refers to a concentration camp and to the slaughter on the beaches of Normandy.) He finds that such juxtapositions of good and evil in this world make God an "incomprehensible" being to mankind.

But the tone of the "Eleven Addresses" is different from the tormented doubt that Henry underwent. The poet tells us here that he has recently, "three weeks ago" (91), undergone a profound religious experience. Echoing Saint Anselm ("I do not seek to understand in order to believe, but I believe in order that I may understand"), the poet says that he does "not understand," but that he still has faith (93). He has said that God is "Unknowable" and has wondered how it is possible to love an unknowable thing (85); but, in the next-to-last prayer, he openly declares his love of God (95). Generally, the tone of Part Four is one of implicit faith in God and praise for Him.

In *Love & Fame,* then, love is seen first as lust, then as friendship and compassion, and finally as a love of God. The poet does not claim to have mastered his lust, but he prays for strength to do so, asking that God protect him from his compulsive venery and that he learn to consider adultery to be as disgusting as incest (88).

The attitude toward fame has similarly undergone a transformation in Part Four. The juxtaposition of fame and lust in Parts One and Two must seem strange until the entire volume is read. Then we come to understand that, just as lust is false love, so also is the desire for fame a distorted motive for art. Inspired by famous poets, the young Berryman egotistically set out to gain fame in the literary world; the Berryman of Part Four finds his inspiration in God and prays that he can forget his desire for literary acclaim. He asks of God that, before he dies, he will have been given the strength to agree with Gerard Manley Hopkins that the only true judge of literature is Christ (95). Keats-like, he longs for love and fame to sink to nothingness. The humility here is completely sincere and forms an astonishing contrast to the braggadocio of many earlier poems.

Love & Fame is, like the *Sonnets* and *The Dream Songs,* another installment of the poet's autobiography in verse. Almost surely the sincerity of Berryman's recovered religious belief will come under question and will become one of the problems in making an ultimate assessment of the man and his work. His faith seems to me to have been at least as hard-earned as Eliot's, Auden's, or Lowell's; but it cannot be certain whether the calm orderliness the poet found through his religious experience would have continued to inform his verse. Several of the poems in *Delusions, etc.* suggest that it might have, for they too are religious poems. But there are also indications in *Delusions, etc.* that the poet's faith was not sufficient to bring him more than a modicum of contentment with this life. The confusions and anxieties of the *Sonnets* and *The Dream Songs* are the characteristic emotions of our time and, in light of the whole body of Berryman's work, of the poet himself.

IV   Delusions, etc.

Berryman's last volume of poems, *Delusions, etc.* (1972) is divided into five sections, but the divisions seem arbitrary rather than structural. The volume does not have a coherent pattern, although the first and last sections achieve some unity by being devoted largely to prayers. All five sections follow various threads of Berryman's persistent subjects; *Love & Fame* succeeded better, however, in weaving a clear design.

The first section, entitled "Opus Dei," begins where *Love & Fame* left off—with a series of hymns to and about God. The poems are titled after the seven canonical hours, from pre-dawn to bedtime. "Lauds" and "Matins" together make up the first of the hours. "Lauds" (3) suggests a strange lack of coherence in itself, for it begins by praising a God of astronomical distances but incongruously turns to the poet's admiration of a new felt hat he has bought for himself. (The word "parsees" in line 4 must be a misprint for "parsecs," units of measurement in astronomy.) "Matins" (4-5) is almost incoherent but refers to the approaching sunrise, with a pun on the words "sun" and "Son," which will alleviate the poet's nightmares and his recollection of his father's death forty years ago. Dawn arrives in "Prime" (6-7). "Interstitial Office" (8), an inserted prayer of social comment, shows the poet at first refusing to kneel because the Minnesota Eight, the group of young draft protesters whom Berryman had written about in *Love & Fame,* had been convicted. He finally submits to God, however, after asking His aid for all of us—especially, it seems, for the judge who presided at the trial of the protesters. The other poems in "Opus Dei" are similar to earlier Berryman poems that express a belief in God and a disbelief in an eternal hell.

Part Two of *Delusions, etc.* is made up of five poems in praise of some Berryman heroes. "Washington in Love" (19) is pretentiously divided into seven lines, each preceded by a roman numeral. The poem alludes among other things to Sarah Cary Fairfax, a neighbor's wife for whom George Washington once declared his love. The first line of the poem contains one of the silly puns of the sort that Berryman occasionally forces upon us: the "terrible upstanding member" is both the awesome and upright Washington and also a private part of him. "Beethoven Triumphant" (20-25), "Your Birthday in Wisconsin You are 140" (26), and "Drugs Alcohol Little Sister" (27) reveal as clearly as did Berryman's study of Stephen Crane that the poet is more interested in biographical details about his heroes than in their art. The poems recite facts about the great composer, about Emily Dickinson, and about Georg Trakl, an Austrian poet who tended toward the wild imagery and nightmarish effects of Expressionism and who also committed suicide in 1914.

The final poem of the second part of *Delusions, etc.* is the best one in the volume. "In Memoriam (1914-1953)" (28-30) recounts Berryman's friendship with Dylan Thomas, who had been born on October 27, 1914, only two days after Berryman. As a joke, Thomas claimed that he had been born one day before Berryman and insisted that Berryman therefore show him the proper respect due one's elders. Berryman seems never to have discovered Thomas's lie, although he knew that the Welshman spun fanciful tales. Several other incidents are referred to—Thomas's attempt to get Berryman drunk on the day he was to meet William Butler Yeats,[5] and Berryman's vigil in Saint Vincent's Hospital in New York, where Thomas lay comatose for five days before he died. In a baffling way, the poem gives us Dylan's name but refers to his wife, Caitlin, as "C——."

Sections Three and Four of *Delusions, etc.* reveal the haphazard make-up of the entire volume. They contain several poems that had been written even before *The Dream Songs* was published. "Scholars at the Orchid Pavilion" (34-35), supposedly a poem about a heaven of Chinese philosophers, had been begun sometime before 1969, as Berryman tells us in the *Harvard Advocate* interview.[6] "The Handshake, The Entrance" (38), "Henry by Night" (52) and "Henry's Understanding" (53) are Dream Songs, and two of them had been published previously.[7] Their themes of insomnia, despair, and anticipated suicide are clear to readers of *The Dream Songs*. Almost incoherently, poems in praise of God and the poem "Hel*lo*" (48), a delightful welcome to Berryman's daughter Sarah Rebecca (born on June 13, 1971), are interspersed with the darker poems of sections Three and Four.

Two poems might better have been placed in the second section of *Delusions, etc.*, where Berryman praised his heroes, than in sections Three and Four. "Lines to Mr Frost"(39) and "Damn You, Jim D., You Woke Me Up" (55) honor two poets. "Jim D." is James Dickey who, before he became a successful poet and critic, wrote advertising copy for the Coca-Cola Company in Atlanta. Berryman mentions the kind words Dickey had written about him in a review of *77 Dream Songs;* he seems not to have read Dickey's revised opinion in the book *Sorties* (1971), where Berryman's life and art are viciously and irresponsibly attacked.[8]

Another poem in Section Three is a further indication that Berryman's last poetry was traveling in uncertain directions. The pessimistic short poem "He Resigns" (40) is strongly influenced by the late poems of Yeats. *Delusions, etc.* suffers from this tendency to mix Berryman styles—the Dream Song stanzas, the Yeatsian quatrains, and the loose quatrains in the manner of *Love & Fame* exist side-by-side in this final volume. The effect is not one of richness of technique but of a confusion of styles; Berryman seems to have been as undecided about his direction as he had been when he was a beginning poet.

The final section of *Delusions, etc.* is, again, similar to the prayerful conclusion to *Love & Fame*. One of the titles, "Unknowable? perhaps not altogether" (60), refers back to an accusation Berryman had made against God in *Love & Fame* (85). The asserted faith in God is modified, however, by the strange and frightening climax of *Delusions, etc.*, for here Berryman does not seem resigned to accept either God's will or life itself. "A Usual Prayer" (62) sounds like *Love & Fame* in its acceptance of God's providence; but the next poem, "Overseas Prayer" (63) mentions Berryman's old anxiety that was initiated by his father's suicide. "Amos" (64) darkly foretells destruction for this world, and with no promise of the redemption that was offered by the Old Testament prophet of the poem's title. "Certainty Before Lunch" (65) seems to reassert God's existence, but it complains about His absence from this world, where the poet is suffering. Berryman gives up his attempts to re-

another by turns, and their rambling on in egotistical or expiatory revelations about the self. The vapidity of the novel can be illustrated by dozens of passages, but one example will suffice. In an encounter session, Severance is told by a doctor to imagine himself as being, of all things, an ampitheater and to explore his subsequent feelings in elaborate detail. After he returns to his room, he continues to analyze himself and begins to write down his impressions:

'It is true that I am only an ampitheatre,' he began. 'But I have a certain power of criticism over the shows that are put on in me. I don't allow shows that are merely entertaining; in fact I insist on shows that are so interesting or difficult that they are put on again and again. Only certain spectators are willing to come so often, but that is quite all right; I am a very ambitious and demanding but not a *greedy* ampitheatre. How about the seats? Not too comfortable, lest somebody drowse, Adjustable? Yes, decidedly; so long as,' Here he broke off bored.

(94)

Severance's boredom in such a passage is shared by his readers.

Except for the first-person passages of Severance's journal, the novel is narrated in third-person point of view. Apparently Berryman was attempting to place some aesthetic distance between himself and his protagonist by the use of the more objective point of view. The attempt fails, for Alan Severance is simply John Berryman by another name. In addition to the several similarities already mentioned, Severance has a penchant for attractive women, has been written up in *Life,* has journeyed to Ireland and to India, attended Columbia and Cambridge, has been thrice married, has a daughter by his third wife and a son by his second, had his first adulterous affair at age thirty-two, and is beset with guilt and anxiety over the death of his father, a member of the National Guard who killed himself when Severance was "twelve." These are only a few of the dozens of correspondences between the novelist and his character. In fact Severance is Berryman, then, in everything except his name and a few incidental details. When Severance, the molecular biologist, discusses with his seminar students the scene in which Polonius gives advice to Laertes, no reader doubts that the arguments are Berryman's.

Other characters and locales are given transparent names: for "Ruth" read Kate, for "David" read Paul, for "Rachel" read

Martha, for "St. Paul's" read South Kent School, and so on. Sometimes Berryman seems to have tired of making up names and calls two of his former professors at Columbia, Casey and Edman, by their actual names (203-05). Again, when they are used at all, the disguises are so flimsy that we must wonder why the entire book was not written in first-person point of view and published as a personal notebook, not as a work of fictional art. Even the parts of the book written in third-person point of view read like the journal of one man's confinement.

Like Severance, the other characters fail to fulfill roles as believable aesthetic creations. Some of these are Jeree, a housewife; Charley B., a hockey pro; George, a guilt-ridden young man; Mike M., an executive married to a beautiful girl and worried whether his old AA chapter, a snobbish one, will re-admit him; Linc, a doctor; Jasper Stone, a bearded poet. All but the last were no doubt people Berryman encountered in hospital. Jasper seems to be another Berryman figure (he has written a book of poems very much like *The Dream Songs*). Jasper corresponds to the friend of Mr. Bones in *The Dream Songs* but is not as important. In *Recovery,* Jasper appears only briefly and disappears about mid-novel. There are at least a score of other characters who appear, are given names, and then are mysteriously dropped. The dust-jacket remarks that the characters "form a cross-section of American life," but in fact they are representative of nothing more than themselves. Unlike those in *The Magic Mountain,* the characters of *Recovery* do not form a microcosm of the outside world, although that may have been Berryman's intention.

The tone of *Recovery* suffers not only from the bathos and narcissism that fill the novel, but also from a kind of private wit that is inappropriate to the book. One of the characters is named "Keg"; another is "Sherry" and she participates in an encounter session with someone named "Vin." Such puns are inconsistent with the serious import of the work.

The theme of *Recovery* seems to have been intended to hinge upon Severance's progression through the twelve steps of the Alcoholics Anonymous program, conveniently listed in the end notes to the novel. But Severance makes no progress as the novel proceeds. He weaves back and forth among the steps, thinking at one time that he may be at step three or at six, and then suddenly feeling that he has taken none of them. Two-thirds of the way through the novel, he feels that he is still "nowhere" (172).

This deflation occurs even after Severance has experienced two incredible epiphanies. At one point he has in exhilaration declared that his whole life has pointed toward a conversion to Judaism (72-74), and feels that Judaism will give him the strength to conquer his alcoholism. This moment of awareness is largely forgotten throughout the rest of the novel as it stands. A second epiphany leads Severance to dedicate his life to medical research, although he seems not to have engaged in any kind of scientific research previously. Two of the discoveries he hopes to make are a cure for cancer and a method of preventing conception that would be both foolproof and acceptable to Catholics (158-59). Berryman presents Severance as being wholly serious and clear-minded in these moments.

Recovery fares somewhat better as an autobiographical document than as a novel. The book has several passages that summarize events in Berryman's life. We are told about the situation behind the *Sonnets* (12-13), his experiences at South Kent (67-69), his father's suicide (191-92, 233), and so on. Such passages occur more frequently in the last third of the book and occasionally contain a biographical detail not available elsewhere.

In his Foreword to *Recovery,* Saul Bellow studiously avoids praising the novel but recalls (sometimes sadly, sometimes fondly) the Berryman he knew. One of the incidents he records makes it clear that recovery would be unavailable to John Berryman in his last years. Berryman had come to Chicago to give a poetry reading. He arrived drunk and alternately shouted and muttered at his listeners. In Bellow's words,

We left a disappointed, bewildered, angry audience. Dignified, he entered a waiting car, sat down, and vomited. He passed out in his room at the Quadrangle Club and slept through the faculty party given in his honor. But in the morning he was full of innocent cheer. He was chirping. It had been a great evening. He recalled an immense success.

(*Recovery,* xiv)

The novelist of *Recovery* seems to have deluded himself also about his last work. The theme of the novel has to do with a man recovering control over his life; but the effect is that of Berryman himself losing control over both his life and his materials. The title *Recovery* is sadly and unintentionally ironic.

CHAPTER *6*

Soundings

JOHN Berryman's career-long search for a style was a quest for the means of expressing an original and forceful personality—a quest that was frustrated in the beginning by the poet's sensitivity to the literary trends of the time. His early verse belongs to the so-called Academic poetry that dominated the American scene in the 1940's and 1950's, a poetry that found its various origins in Yeats, Eliot, and Auden. It is a poetry restrained in emotion, formal and level in tone, traditional in form (or at least consciously dependent upon traditional devices), polished in technique, symbolic in import. The poet of such verse became a Joycean god-creator, paring his fingernails, refined almost out of existence. Berryman wrote some memorable verse in this tradition—"Winter Landscape," "The Dispossessed," and a few others—and in the early poetry he had focused on the themes that he would later develop.

But he clearly had not found his own voice even in the best of these poems. That does not mean that he had failed to master a style—or several styles. William J. Martz implies that Berryman's early work, and most of it afterward, demonstrates an "unevenness" that is largely a failure of style.[1] Rather, the early poems reveal a mastery of several styles at once, all of them Academic: the Yeats-Auden style of Berryman's "Boston Common," the clear and direct style of his "Winter Landscape," and the symbolically complex style of his "The Dispossessed." Berryman could have chosen to continue writing poems like these and no doubt would have remained a respected but distinctly minor poet in the Academic tradition. Like most Academics, he would be praised for his control and technique but adversely criticized for a lack of blood, of spontaneity, and of personality. Instead, he chose to take great risks with style and with his own psyche.

Berryman's Sonnets, the first result of such risks, forthrightly present a dissociated personality in a style of distorted syntax and nervous energy that is uniquely Berryman's. The *Sonnets* are personal poetry that becomes universal by virtue of the story they present—the archetypal one of David and Bathsheba or Paolo and Francesca. The *Sonnets* solved the problem of personality for Berryman, but they were written at a time when intensely personal poetry was taboo in this country. The sonnet form in itself misled some reviewers into assuming that the poems were merely an exercise in technique; in fact, the poems are moving expressions of Berryman's deepest emotions of obsessive love, guilt, and despair. They too may be called "uneven," but only in the way that any long sequence cannot be comprised of poems of equal merit. Curiously, of a total of twenty-seven *Sonnets* that four reviewers have listed as the best ones of the sequence, only two (32 and 115) are found on more than one list.[2] Perhaps the critics praised the *Sonnets* they understood and ignored the others. No more than a score of the *Sonnets* are notably weak, and I include in that number certain ones (38, 109, and others) I find baffling because they contain allusions I have been unable to ferret out.

Berryman realized, long before the *Sonnets* were published, that he would have to invent stanzaic patterns of his own if he were to be taken seriously; and *Homage to Mistress Bradstreet* was the result. Although risky in technique, the poem risks nothing of the poet's self. The stanza form and the strained, elliptical style were thoroughly original; but Berryman failed to find the means in *Homage* of clarifying his theme of the poet's relationship to America. He seems to have begun with the generalities "Poet" and "America" rather than with himself as a poet; *Homage* became abstract and difficult in ways that the *Sonnets* and *The Dream Songs* are not. Hiding behind the mask of Anne Bradstreet, Berryman tells us almost nothing about himself. *Homage* represents, in my view, the dead-end of purely Academic verse for Berryman. Its technical control, its heavily suggestive and symbolic manner, its impersonality and formality found an appreciative audience among some of the literati but nowhere else. Only in its style and in its originality of form does it compare with *The Dream Songs*.

The poet began writing Dream Songs a year or two after completing *Homage,* and he found in them his voice and manner. He was nearly forty years old, the age Robert Frost mentions somewhere as the upper limit for a poet who is ever going to find his way. Again, Berryman was in the center of the poetic currents of his time, and farther downstream than most, as can best be understood by a glance at the contemporaneous trends in poetry. During the 1950's in America arose the rebellion of the Beat poets against Academic verse, a revolt led by Allen Ginsberg. The Beats felt that the Academics' emphasis upon technique resulted in a bloodless, cerebral, artificial poetry. Misreading their cues from Walt Whitman, William Carlos Williams, and E. E. Cummings, the Beats insisted upon Life and Truth rather than upon Art. They considered form irrelevant and restraint unnecessary, and they allowed their expansive emotionalism to include all levels of language and all kinds of subject matter, although they tended toward a colloquial language spoken by an all-important Self. The movement produced some fine poems and much balderdash, and probably had an influence—although they might deny it—upon several Academic poets. Or it may be that Academic poetry had run its course, that poets felt too restricted by the objectivity that Eliot had insisted upon and chose to move towards a more personal art.

Surely Berryman had begun to write Dream Songs before he had a chance to read much, if any, Beat poetry. In any case by 1959, with the publication of Robert Lowell's *Life Studies,* Academic poets were taking avenues that the Beats had also traveled. The personal note in Lowell's poetry was concurrently struck by Berryman, who began to publish individual Dream Songs in the same year that *Life Studies* appeared. Other poets of controlled technique followed or contributed to the trend—Sylvia Plath and W. D. Snodgrass very successfully; Anne Sexton with dubious results. The Beats and their descendants seem to have avoided any counterinfluence by the Academics. Beat poetry remains an unformed cry; the Beats ignore technical control, apparently because they fear that it may falsify Experience.

The Dream Songs successfully combine the best of these two tendencies of modern verse. They are in the mainstream of poetry in their demonstrated mastery of technique and in their continual return to a metrical pattern—qualities that are likely to remain essential to poetry in English. At the same time, they are deeply felt and apparently spontaneous embodiments of experience; and no one could call them bloodless. Their range of emotion is wide and behind them, or in them, is the personality of the poet, fully expressed yet seldom maudlin or narcissistic. Berryman achieves a suitable aesthetic distance in the Songs by the device of the mask and by the use of various pronouns to designate the protagonist, but the effect is never one of the poet's hiding behind his work. He is not a disembodied personality, nor is Henry an artificially created one.

The unevenness that Berryman was accused of is illustrated by his last poems, *Love & Fame* and *Delusions, etc.* For whatever reasons, these poems are more directly personal than the Dream Songs: the mask has been dropped, and the poet speaks to us in the first person. The movement toward personal poetry or confessional poetry probably will continue for some years, but some of the passages in the last two volumes demonstrate the dangers it must avoid. In confessional poetry, honesty too easily becomes embarrassing self-revelation or vulgarity; and the poet can too easily assume that his private experiences are universals.

In *The Dream Songs* the individual became the archetype of modern man, or at least of the modern poet. Lost in an existential world, living on the edge of madness, Henry saw all of the world and saw it fragmented; he suffered and yet could also see that his situation and ours, whatever its difficulty, has moments of joy and humor and consolation. But in *Love & Fame* the individual poet remains only himself. One reviewer feels that the "I" of the poems is transformed into the universal man as *Love & Fame* proceeds,[3] but the work seems to me autobiographical in extreme ways that the *Sonnets* and *The Dream Songs* are not. It may be that the theme of *Love & Fame*—the love of God replacing lust and a desire for literary recognition—is, like the theme of the *Sonnets,* sufficiently generalized to rescue the poems from narcissism. Even if it is, the movement from existential despair to religious belief is not a direction that most men or most poets can take in our time, in spite of the examples of Eliot and Auden.

In reading *Love & Fame* or *Delusions, etc.,* we must wonder why Berryman discarded some traditional beliefs—in the afterlife, for example—and yet insisted on others. It would seem simpler to accept all, in faith, or to reject the whole system. This question is only one of many that need a fuller analysis by critics, particularly by critics with a psychological bent. Whether they can answer that question is uncertain; but the use of Freudian psychology in analyzing Berryman's poetry and his personality is likely to be more revealing and less speculative than such criticism usually is, for Berryman's own interest in Freudian theory informs much of his poetry and is an essential part of his world view. Critics may deplore the application of such a method when it is used to analyze writers who are themselves ignorant of psychology, but in Berryman's case it would be a valid approach and would offer many insights.

It is premature to speculate about Berryman's ultimate place in poetry. Of the poets whom he must be placed alongside—Robert Lowell, Karl Shapiro, Richard Wilbur, Theodore Roethke—all but the last are still alive and writing well. It is possible, however, to gauge the present view of Berryman's accomplishments. Since his poetry tends to elicit either enthusiasm or repulsion,[4] judgments about his work vary widely. At present the early poetry is considered derivative, the *Sonnets* and *Homage* are usually viewed as qualified successes, and *The Dream Songs* are seen as the poet's major work and have received widespread critical approval, some of it lavish. A. Poulin has noted that, on the basis of *The Dream Songs,* Berryman "has already been compared to Whitman and Homer and Dante. Of course, this will have to be borne out by a closer examination of his work, but a superficial examination seems to indicate that he may have constructed . . . a work that is at least equivalent to 'The Waste Land.' "[5] Not all reviewers would agree; some have called the Songs simply confused and confusing. We may recall that the catch-cry of "incomprehensible" was raised against Eliot and Joyce only a few years ago, but Prufrock and Leopold Bloom are now familiar figures to undergraduates. I suspect the same will happen to Henry.

It is safe to say that *The Dream Songs* are likely for some time to be considered the most important poetry published in America during the 1960's. Possibly these Songs will become a standard literary work of the century—they deserve to because of their success in embodying large areas of poetic and human experience in a style that is original, definitive, and thoroughly memorable.

Notes and References

Chapter One

1. *Homage to Mistress Bradstreet* was first published in *Partisan Review*, XX (Sept.-Oct. 1953), 489-503, and then reprinted in book form (New York: Farrar, Straus & Cudahy, 1956). The edition used in this study, hereinafter cited internally as *Homage,* is *Homage to Mistress Bradstreet and Other Poems* (New York, 1968).

2. *His Thought Made Pockets & the Plane Buckt* (Pawlet, Vermont, 1958). This volume was reprinted in *Short Poems* (New York, 1967), hereinafter cited internally.

3. *Berryman's Sonnets* (New York, 1967); Hereinafter cited internally as *Sonnets.*

4. As quoted in Jane Howard's article, "Whisky and Ink, Whisky and Ink," *Life* (July 21, 1967), p. 74.

5. *The Dream Songs* (New York, 1969); hereinafter cited internally by Song number rather than by page.

6. *Love & Fame* (New York, 1970); *Delusions, etc.* (New York, 1972); hereinafter cited internally.

7. E.G., *Current Biography,* XXX (May 1969), 6, incorrectly list Berryman's father as "John Allen Smith Berryman."

8. Howard, p. 74.

9. John Berryman, "An Interview with John Berryman," *Harvard Advocate,* CIII (Spring 1969), 4.

10. John Berryman, in a letter to me dated June 6, 1970.

11. William J. Martz, *John Berryman,* University of Minnesota Pamphlets on American Writers, No. 85 (Minneapolis, 1969), pp. 5-6. Martz writes me (in a letter of May 11, 1970) that the biographical information in his study was taken from an interview with Berryman in October 1968.

12. As quoted in Howard, p. 74. An indication of Berryman's amnesia is found in his confusion about his age at the time of his father's death. He usually said that he was twelve when it occurred but in fact he was eleven.

13. Berryman, "An Interview," p.5.

14. *Ibid.,* p.4.

15. Lester Wittenberg, Jr., in a letter to me dated March 11, 1970.

16. Berryman, "An Interview," p. 4.

17. Wittenberg, letter of March 11, 1970.

18. Martz, p. 6.

19. Wittenberg, letter of March 11, 1970.

20. Martz, p. 6.

21. Wittenberg, letter of March 11, 1970.

22. *Ibid.*

23. Martz, p. 6.

24. Wittenberg, letter of March 11, 1970.

25. Berryman, letter of June 6, 1970. Dream Song 70 and the short story "The Imaginary Jew," *Kenyon Review,* VII (Autumn 1945), 529-39, refer to Berryman's rowing experiences.

26. Martz, p. 7.

27. Berryman, "An Interview," p. 5.

28. Mark Van Doren, "John Berryman," *Harvard Advocate,* CIII (Spring 1969), 17.

29. Berryman, "An Interview," p. 5.

30. *Ibid.*

31. CXLI, (July 10, 1935), 38.

32. For Berryman's reaction to the prejudice he observed during his Columbia days, see especially the poem "Nowhere," *Love & Fame,* p. 20, and the story "The Imaginary Jew."

33. Howard, p. 74.

34. Martz, p. 7.

35. The location is specified in John Berryman's *Poems* (Norfolk, Conn., 1940), p. 13; hereinafter cited internally. The date "1939" is given in *Short Poems,* p. 41.

36. Biographical note in John Berryman's "Twenty Poems," *Five Young American Poets* (Norfolk, Conn., 1940), p. 43; hereinafter cited internally.

37. Berryman points out that the incident occurred essentially as it is presented in the story ("An Interview," p. 6).

38. "The Imaginary Jew." p. 534.

39. "The Lovers," *Kenyon Review,* VII (Winter 1945), 1-11.

40. *The Dispossessed* (New York, 1948). Reprinted in *Short Poems* (1967).

41. *Stephen Crane* (New York, 1950). The edition hereinafter cited internally is a paperback reprint (Cleveland, Ohio, 1962). The reprint retains the same pagination but has a second preface added by Berryman.

42. Berryman's assessment was disputed by several reviewers; one was Granville Hicks, "Three Men of Letters," *Sewanee Review,* LX (Winter 1952), 154.

43. John T. Flanagan was irritated by this sentence ("Stephen Crane," *American Literature,* XXIII (1951), 511); other reviewers found numerous

examples of stylistic awkwardness.

44. As quoted by Graham Greene, one of the few reviewers who found *Stephen Crane* wholly unsatisfactory ("The Badge of Courage," *New Statesman and Nation*, XLI [June 2, 1951], 627-28).

45. Edwin Cady, *Stephen Crane* (New York, 1962), p. 170.

46. Martz, p. 10. The reviewer was Morgan Blum, "Berryman as Biographer, Stephen Crane as Poet," *Poetry*, LXXVIII (August 1951), 302.

47. Reviewers have questioned whether Crane actually had the suicidal impulses Berryman attributes to him, and whether the stabbing incident is as important as Berryman makes it out to be.

48. Howard, p. 68.

49. Berryman, "An Interview," p. 9.

50. *Ibid.*, p.73.

51. *Ibid., passim.*

52. *Ibid.*, p. 76. The poet noted, however, in a letter to me dated June 27, 1971, that this affair was the first to occur in his "then 5-year-old marriage" to Eileen.

53. Monroe Engel, "An Educational Incident," *Harvard Advocate*, CIII (Spring 1969), 18.

54. Martz, p. 7.

55. *Ibid.*, p. 8.

56. Richard J. Kelly, *John Berryman: a Checklist* (Metuchen, N.J. 1972), p. xxxv.

57. Martz, p. 8.

58. Kelly, p. xxxv.

59. Howard, p. 70.

60. *Ibid.*

61. Berryman, "An Interview," p. 8.

62. Howard, p. 75.

63. John Berryman, *Recovery* (New York, 1973); hereinafter cited internally.

Chapter Two

1. John Berryman, "One Answer to a Question," *Shenandoah*, XVII (Autumn 1965), 68.

2. Berryman explicated this poem fully in "A Note on Poetry," "Twenty Poems," pp. 45-48.

3. Berryman, "One Answer," p. 72.

4. Cf. Dream Song 254, where the poet mentions being kicked in the face as he tackled a player at South Kent.

5. The poet has pointed out that the first line of this poem is a variation of Delmore Schwartz's "Tired and Unhappy, You Think of Houses" (*The Dispossessed*, vii).

6. "Waiting for the End, Boys," *Partisan Review*, XVV (Feb. 1948), 254.

7. When first collected, in "Twenty Poems," 75-76, the poem was titled "The Return."

8. The date that follows the poem, "11 May 1939," is incorrect.

9. Dudley Fitts, "Deep in the Unfriendly City," *New York Times Book Review,* June 20, 1948, p. 4.

10. Pearl Strachan, "The World of Poetry," *Christian Science Monitor,* Weekly Magazine Section, Oct. 3, 1942, p. 10.

11. According to Monroe K. Spears (*The Poetry of W.H. Auden* [New York, 1968], p. 356), Auden's poem was first published on Oct. 18, 1939. Berryman also seems to have written his poem very soon after the events; by its placement in Poems, *it was written before "Communist," which is dated "October 1939"* (Poems, *15*).

12. Robert Fitzgerald, "Poetry and Perfection," *Sewanee Review,* LVI (Autumn 1948), 692.

13. Berryman furnished the information about Teng Fa and Tracy Doll in a letter to me dated June 27, 1971.

14. Berryman mentions "the mounted man" as an unrivaled "symbol for power" in his short story "The Imaginery Jew," p. 533.

15. Much of the poem's diction is from William James's speech, which can be found in *Memories and Studies* (New York, 1968), pp. 37-61.

16. Samuel French Morse, "Twelve Poets," *Virginia Quarterly Review,* XLIV (Summer 1968), 510.

17. Fitts, p. 4.

18. Berryman, "One Answer," p. 69. *cf.* Ezra Pound's "The Return."

19. Robert Lowell, "The Poetry of John Berryman," *New York Review of Books,* II (May 28, 1964), p.3.

20. Berryman, "One Answer," p. 69. "Winter Landscape" was first published in *The New Republic,* CVIII (July 8, 1940); Auden's "Musee des Beaux Arts" first appeared in *New Writing (Spring 1939). Spears,* The Poetry of W.H. Auden, *p. 348.*

21. Arthur and Catherine Evans, "Pieter Bruegel and John Berryman: Two Winter Landscapes," *Texas Studies in Language and Literature,* V (Autumn 19630, 309.

22. Berryman, "One Answer," pp. 69-70

23. *Ibid.,* p. 70.

24. Martz, p. 18.

25. Lowell, p. 3.

26. Berryman, "One Answer," p. 68.

27. Ian Hamilton first noted the similarity in "John Berryman," *London Magazine,* IV (Feb. 1965), 94.

28. *Ibid.,* p. 95.

29. The cause of Campbell's death is specified in Dream Song 88.

30. John Frederick Nims, "World's Fair," *Poetry: A Critical Supplement* (April 1948), p. 6.

31. Martz, p. 6.

32. *Ibid.*, p. 7.

33. John Berryman, *Poet's Choice,* ed. Paul Engle and Joseph Langland (New York, 1962), p. 135.

34. Nims, "The Dispossessed," *Poetry,* pp. 1-5.

35. John Berryman, "The State of American Writing: 1948," *Partisan Review,* XV (Aug. 1949), 857.

36. Berryman, as quoted in Howard, p. 76.

37. Lowell, p. 34.

38. The allusions in "Cloud and Flame" are to Swift, who because of his distaste for scholastic philosophy was permitted to graduate from Trinity College, Dublin, only by special arrangement; to John Cornford, a British poet killed in Spain in 1936; and to Thirkill (or Thurkill) the Sacrist who observed a statue of Christ bow its head before King Harold of England, indicating that Harold would be killed in the Battle of Hastings. *American Poetry,* ed. Gay Wilson Allen, Walter E. Rideout, and James K. Robinson (New York, 1965), n., p. 1075.

39. See John Berryman, "The Poetry of Ezra Pound," *Partisan Review,* XVI (April 1949), 389; and "An Interview with John Berryman," *Harvard Advocate,* CIII (Spring 1969), 5. The Pound article was intended as the introduction to *Ezra Pound: Selected Poems* (New York: New Directions, 1949), but it was rejected by Pound and by James Laughlin as being unsuitable for "young readers." In a letter to me dated June 27, 1971, Berryman wrote that his selection of Pound's poems may also have been discarded for the same reason — he is not certain, for he never looked at the published volume to see which poems it contains. New Directions is noncommittal on the matter.

40. Berryman, "The Poetry of Ezra Pound," p. 388.

41. Berryman, "One Answer," P. 71.

42. Martz, p. 17.

43. *Ibid.*

44. William Meredith, "Henry Tasting All the Secret Bits of Life: Berryman's Dream Songs," *Wisconsin Studies in Contemporary Literature,* VI (Winter-Spring 1965), 27.

Chapter Three

1. Berryman, "An Interview," pp. 7-8.

2. William Meredity, "A Bright Surviving Actual Scene: Berryman's Sonnets," *Harvard Advocate,* CIII (Spring 1969). 21.

3. Stephen Stepanchev, "Berryman's Sonnets," *New Leader,* L (May 22, 1967), 26.

4. Berryman, "An Interview," p. 7.

5. X.J. Kennedy, *An Introduction to Poetry* (Boston, 1966), p. 184.

6. E.G., Peter A. Stitt, "Berryman's Vein Profound," *Minnesota Review,* VII (1967), 357.

7. Berryman, "One Answer," p. 74.

8. Elizabeth Wade White, Review of *Homage to Mistress Bradstreet, New England Quarterly,* XXIX (Dec. 1956), 547.

9. Anne Bradstreet, as quoted in Alan Holder, "Anne Bradstreet Resurrected," *Concerning Poetry,* II (Spring 1969), 15. Holder says that Berryman "appears to have appropriated the account found in Campbell of a contemporary of Anne's . . ." who was left deformed by smallpox (15).

10. White, pp. 545, 547.

11. Robert Lowell, "The Poetry of John Berryman," *New York Review of Books,* II (May 28, 1964), 3. Lowell may have been praising too the wide diversity of the sources of the poem, from original documents to Paul Klee and Graham Greene, (*Homage,* n., pp. 30-31).

12. Berryman, "An Interview," p. 7.

13. Berryman, "One Answer," p. 73.

14. Berryman, "An Interview, p. 7.

15. Anne Bradstreet, *The Works of Anne Bradstreet,* ed. John Harvard Ellis (New York, 1932), p. 101.

16. Berryman, "One Answer," p. 73.

17. Howard, p. 74.

18. Berryman, "One Answer," pp. 73-74.

19. *Ibid.,* p. 74.

20. Helen Vendler, "Savage, Rueful, Irrepressible Henry," *New York Times Book Review,* Nov. 3, 1968, pp. 1, 58.

21. Berryman, "One Answer," p. 72.

22. John Thompson, "An Alphabet of Poets," *New York Review of Books,* XI (Aug. 1, 1968), 34.

23. John Ciardi, "The Researched Mistress," *Saturday Review,* XL (Mar. 23, 1957), 36.

24. Berryman, "One Answer," p. 72.

25. Berryman, as quoted in Howard, p. 74.

26. Berryman, "An Interview," p. 7.

Chapter Four

1. Berryman, "An Interview," p. 7.

2. Berryman, letter of June 6, 1970.

3. *Ibid.*

4. Lowell, p. 3.

5. Berryman, "An Interview," p. 6.

6. *Ibid.* Berryman insisted that he did not take the name "Henry" from

Stephen Crane, who was fascinated with it (*Stephen Crane,* pp. 214, 310-11, 324-25).

7. Berryman, "One Answer," p. 67.

8. Berryman, "An Interview," p. 5.

9. Martz, p. 36.

10. Berryman, "An Interview," p. 6.

11. William Wasserstrom, "Cagey John: Berryman as Medicine Man," *Centennial Review,* XII (Summer 1968), 336-38.

12. Berryman, "An Interview," p. 6. Berryman admired men of heroic action as much as did Yeats; Henry praises the O'Rahilly, Connolly, and Pearse (309), and adds to the master's list such names as those of the explorers Andree, Fraenkl, and Strindberg (11).

13. Wasserstrom, p. 338.

14. Berryman tells us in "An Interview," p. 9, that he read "The Madman in the Tower," *Time* (Aug. 12, 1966), pp. 14-19.

15. Berryman, "The Poetry of Ezra Pound," pp. 388-94.

16. Van Doren's comment about "being found out" was, then, a remark that Frost himself had made in an earlier conversation. In a letter, Frost had once expressed the fear of being around "literary people for too long a time at the risk of losing their respect by being found out . . ." (*The Letters of Robert Frost to Louis Untermeyer* [New York, 1963], p. 271.)

17. Most of the details in the first two stanzas of the Song are factual. On September 17, 1922, the Reverend Mr. Edward Wheeler Hall and his lover, Mrs. Eleanor Mills, were found murdered under a crab-apple tree on a farm in New Jersey. He had been shot once in the head; she was shot three times and her throat was slit. The bodies had then been laid together, and Mrs. Mills's love letters were strewn over the pair. Berryman probably imagined the detail of the murderers' being dressed in white sheets. A "flashlight" and Mrs. Mills's screaming were mentioned in testimony at the 1926 trial of Mrs. Hall and her two brothers. They were acquitted, and the murderers were never found. See Paul Sann, "The Murder in Lovers Lane," *The Lawless Decade* (New York, 1957), pp. 142-48.

18. Berryman, "An Interview," p. 6.

19. *Ibid.*

20. Carl Wittke, *Tambo and Bones* (Durham, North Carolina, 1930), *passim.* Wasserstrom first noted this influence on Berryman.

21. Berryman, "An Interview," p. 6.

22. Wittke, p. 164.

23. Wasserstrom, p. 343.

24. Christ "was not born" on Christmas day only because the birthday and year are uncertain, as Berryman says in Song 234 ("The Carpenter's Son").

25. Berryman, as quoted in Howard, p. 74.

26. Berryman, "An Interview," p. 7.

27. *Ibid.,* p. 8.

28. Berryman's relatively sympathetic view of Nixon in the unquoted last stanza of this Song (he is said to be brave and intelligent) had changed to detestation by 1970. See the poem "The American Hero," *New York Review of Books* (Oct. 8, 1970), p. 6.

29. Berryman, "The Poetry of Ezra Pound," p. 394.

30. W. D. Snodgrass, *Poet's Choice,* ed. Paul Engle and Joseph Langland (New York, 1962), p. 248.

31. Wasserstrom, p. 352, first noted the passage as relevant to Henry's performance.

32. Berryman, "Waiting for the End, Boys," pp. 265-66.

33. Berryman, "The State of American Writing, 1948: Seven Questions," pp. 858-59.

34. Berryman, "An Interview," p. 9.

35. Blaise Pascal, *Pensées* [and] *The Provincial Letters,* trans. W. F. Trotter and Thomas M'Crie (New York, 1941), pp. 64-85.

36. Berryman, "An Interview," p. 9.

37. Berryman, letter of June 6, 1970.

38. Martz, p. 15.

39. Berryman, "A Tribute," *Agenda,* IV (Oct.-Nov. 1966), 27.

40. Sigmund Freud, *A General Introduction to Psychoanalysis,* trans. Joan Riviere (Garden City, N.Y., 1953), p. 164.

41. Berryman, "An Interview," p. 5.

42. Sigmund Freud, *Freud: Dictionary of Psychoanalysis,* ed. Nandor Fodor and Frank Gaynor (New York, 1958), p. 17.

43. The image of a man with a wooden leg occurred in "The Captain's Song" (*Short Poems,* 72.).

44. Berryman, "An Interview," p. 6.

45. The word "survive," in one form or another, occurs frequently in Berryman's work—for example, in the early poem "Surviving Love" (*Short Poems,* 77), where the word means "living over" illicit love, not a love that "survives."

46. Martz, p. 7.

47. Jarrell's review is "Verse Chronicle," *Nation,* CLXVII (July 17, 1948), 80-81. The source for 1939 as the beginning year of Berryman's acquaintance with Jarrell is Berryman's "Randall Jarrell," *Randall Jarrell: 1914-1965,* ed. Robert Lowell, Peter Taylor, and Robert Penn Warren (New York, 1967), p. 10.

48. Carlos Baker, *Ernest Hemingway: A Life Story* (New York, 1969), p. 598.

49. Henry's reference to Leopold Bloom in a Song (288) in which suicide is considered may be another allusion to the suicide of a father;

Bloom's father, Rudolph Virag, had also killed himself, although not with a gun.

50. Marz, p. 6.

51. Card-playing is a frequent image in *The Dream Songs*. The third epigraph to *His Toy, His Dream, His Rest* quotes a letter from Keats to Shelley: "I am pickt up and sorted to a pip" ("pips" are the spots on playing cards). Henry plays cards several times, perhaps because he gambles with life and death or because he views life and poetry as competitive processes.

52. Berryman, "An Interview," p. 8.

53. *Ibid.*

54. Berryman, "The Poetry of Ezra Pound," p. 391.

55. Berryman, "An Interview," p. 8.

56. Karl Shapiro and Robert Beum, *A Prosody Handbook* (New York, 1965), p. 90.

57. Robert Hillyer, *First Principles of Verse* (Boston, 1938), p. 29.

58. Frederick Seidel, "Berryman's Dream Songs," *Poetry,* CV (Jan. 1965), 259.

59. Berryman, "Waiting for the End, Boys," p. 263.

60. Meredith, "Henry Tasting All," p. 31.

61. *Ibid.,* p. 29.

62. Berryman, "One Answer," p. 76. The two reviewers were Robert Lowell, p. 4, and Adrienne Rich, "Mrs. Bones, He Lives," *Nation,* CXCVIII (May 25, 1964), p. 540. One final example of the mixed tone of *The Dream Songs* is the title of *His Toy, His Dream, His Rest.* Ambiguously, the "toy" is both penis and poetry; the "dream" is a desire for females and fame; the "rest" is sex (or its aftermath) and death.

63. As quoted in Philip Toynbee's review, "Berryman's Songs," *Encounter,* XXIV (Mar. 1965), 77.

64. *Ibid.,* pp. 76-78.

65. Carol Johnson first drew the analogy between the infectious styles of Hemingway and *The Dream Songs,* and warned Berryman against "the temptation to become his own parodist" ("John Berryman: The Dream songs," *Harvard Advocate,* CIII [Spring 1969], 25).

Chapter Five

1. Readers interested in numerology may note that the 385 Dream Songs plus the 59 poems of *Love & Fame* total 444, a triple magic number.

2. Daniel Jaffe, "A Shared Language in the Poet's Tongue," *Saturday Review,* LIV (April 3, 1971), 31.

3. One reviewer has suggested that the poems have taken sections of Ezra

Pounds's "Hugh Selwyn Mauberley" as their model (William H. Pritchard, "Love & Fame," *New York Times Book Review,* Jan. 24, 1971, p. 5).

4.   "The Poetry of John Berryman," *New York Review of Books* (May 28, 1964), p. 3.
5.   This is the same incident mentioned in Sonnet 5 and in Dream Songs 88, 215, and 218.
6.   Berryman, "An Interview" p. 8.
7.   John Berryman, "Henry's Understanding," "Henry by Night," *Harvard Advocate,* CIII (Spring 1969), 12-13.
8.   James Dickey's review of *77 Dream Songs* was first published in *The American Scholar,* XXXIV (Autumn 1965), 648, and reprinted in his *Babel to Byzantium: Poets & Poetry Now* (New York, 1968), pp. 198-99. His negative opinions are found in *Sorties* (Garden City, New York, 1971), pp. 52, 85, 101.

Chapter Six

1.   Martz, pp. 5, 8-9, 17-18.
2.   The four are Martz, p. 25; Albert Gelpi, "Early Poems by Berryman," *Christian Science Monitor,* July 20, 1967, p. 5; Stephen Stepanchev, "Berryman's Sonnets," *The New Leader,* L (May 22, 1967), 26; and Peter A. Stitt, "Berryman's Vein Profound," *Minnesota Review,* VII (1967), 356.
3.   Jaffe, p. 31.
4.   A. Alvarez, "John Berryman," *Beyond All This Fiddle* (London, 1968), p. 88.
5.   A. Poulin, "An Interview with A. Poulin, Jr.," *English News,* January 1971, p. 5.

Selected Bibliography

PRIMARY SOURCES

1. Poetry

Berryman's Sonnets. New York: Farrar, Straus & Giroux, 1967.
Delusions, etc. New York: Farrar, Straus & Giroux, 1972.
The Dispossessed. New York: William Sloane Associates, 1948.
The Dream Songs. New York: Farrar, Straus & Giroux, 1969. (A combined edition of 77 *Dream Songs* and *His Toy, His Dream, His Rest.*)
His Thought Made Pockets & the Plane Buckt. Pawlet, Vermont: C. Fredericks, 1958.
His Toy, His Dream, His Rest: 308 Dream Songs. New York: Farrar, Straus & Giroux, 1968.
Homage to Mistress Bradstreet. New York: Farrar, Straus & Giroux, 1956.
Homage to Mistress Bradstreet and Other Poems. New York: Farrar, Straus & Giroux, 1968. (Includes *Homage* and selections from *The Dispossessed* and *His Thought Made Pockets & the Plane Buckt.*)
Love & Fame. New York: Farrar, Straus & Giroux, 1970.
Poems. Norfolk, Conn.: New Directions, 1942.
77 Dream Songs. New York: Farrar, Straus & Giroux, 1964.
Short Poems. New York: Farrar, Straus & Giroux, 1967. (Contains *The Dispossessed, His Thought Made Pockets & The Plane Buckt,* and "Formal Elegy.")
"Twenty Poems," *Five Young American Poets.* Norfolk, Conn.: New Directions, 1940.

2. Prose

"The Art of Poetry XVI," *Paris Review,* XIV (Winter 1972), 177-207.
With Ralph Ross and Allen Tate. *The Arts of Reading.* New York: Thomas Y. Crowell, 1960.
"Despondency and Madness: On Robert Lowell's 'Skunk Hour.' " *The Contemporary Poet as Artist and Critic.* Ed. Anthony Ostroff. Boston: Little, Brown, 1964.
"F. Scott Fitzgerald," *Kenyon Review,* VIII (Winter 1946), 103-12.

"The Imaginary Jew," *Kenyon Review,* VII (Autumn 1945), 529-39.

"An Interview with John Berryman," *Harvard Advocate,* CIII (Spring 1969), 4-9

"The Long Way to MacDiarmid," *Poetry,* LXXXVIII (April 1956), 52-61.

"The Loud Hill of Wales," *Kenyon Review,* II (Autumn 1940), 481-85.

"The Lovers," *Kenyon Review,* VII (Winter 1945), 1-11.

"Lowell, Thomas, & C.," *Partisan Review,* XIV (Jan.-Feb. 1947), 73-83.

"From the Middle and Senior Generations," *American Scholar,* XXVIII (Summer 1959), 384-90.

"A Note on Poetry," *Five Young American Poets.* Norfolk, Conn.: New Directions, 1940.

"One Answer to a Question," *Shenandoah,* XVII (Autumn 1965), 67-76.

"On Poetry and the Age" and "Randall Jarrell." *Randall Jarrell: 1914-1965.* Ed. Robert Lowell, Peter Taylor, and Robert Penn Warren. New York: Farrar, Straus & Giroux, 1967.

"The Poetry of Ezra Pound," *Partisan Review,* XVI (April 1949), 377-94.

Recovery. New York: Farrar, Straus & Giroux, 1973.

"Shakespeare at Thirty," *Hudson Review,* VI (Summer 1953), 175-203.

"Spender: The Poet as Critic," *New Republic,* CXLVIII (June 29, 1963), 19-20.

"The State of American Writing, 1948: Seven Questions," *Partisan Review,* XV (August 1948), 855-60.

Stephen Crane. New York: William Sloane Associates, 1950. (Reprinted with a second preface, Cleveland: World Publishing, Meridian, 1962.)

"Stephen Crane: The Red Badge of Courage." *The American Novel from James Fenimore Cooper to William Faulkner.* Ed. Wallace Stegner. New York: Basic Books, 1965.

"Three and a Half Years at Columbia." *University on the Heights.* Ed. Wesley First. New York: Doubleday, 1969.

"A Tribute [to Ezra Pound]," *Agenda,* IV (October-November 1966), 27-28.

"Waiting for the End, Boys," *Partisan Review,* XV (February 1948), 254-67.

"Young Poets Dead," *Sewanee Review,* LV (July-September 1947), 504-14.

3. Editions and Introductions

DREISER, THEODORE. *The Titan.* Afterword by John Berryman. New York: New American Library, 1965.

LEWIS, MATTHEW G. *The Monk.* Ed. Louis F. Peck. Introduction by John Berryman. New York: Grove Press, 1952.

NASHE, THOMAS. *The Unfortunate Traveller, or, The Life of Jack Wilton.* Ed. with an introduction by John Berryman. New York: Putnam's, 1960.

POUND, EZRA. *Ezra Pound: Selected Poems*. [Ed. John Berryman?]. New York: New Directions, 1949.

SECONDARY SOURCES

ALVAREZ, A[LFRED]. *Beyond All This Fiddle*. London: Penguin, 1968. Places Berryman in the center of twentieth-century movements in art and poetry, particularly in what Alvarez calls an "Extremist" style—personal, an "extension of Romanticism," requiring full "internal resources," a style that is a "courageous response" to an age of fragmentation.

"An American Poet." Anon. review of *The Dispossessed, Times Literary Supplement* (London), July 3, 1948, p. 374. Finds the poems to be "not always brilliant, [but] always thoughtful and friendly, and [to] invite re-reading." Judges Berryman and young American poets generally to be superior to their British counterparts.

"Badge of Courage." Anon. review of *Stephen Crane, Times Literary Supplement* (London), June 8, 1951, p. 356. Ironic and arch attack on Berryman's Freudian approach.

BEACH, JOSEPH WARREN,. "Five Makers of American Fiction," *Yale Review*, XL (June 1951), 744-47. Criticizes the "insensitiveness" of the style of *Stephen Crane* but praises the Freudian analysis of Crane's personality.

BLUM, MORGAN. "Berryman as Biographer, Stephen Crane as Poet," *Poetry*, LXXVIII (August 1951), 298-307. Balanced judgment that *Stephen Crane* is both "flawed and distinguished."

CARRUTH, HAYDEN. "Declining Occasions," *Poetry*, CXII (May 1968), 119-21. Finds the *Sonnets* to be the stylistic forerunner of *The Dream Songs*, and prefers them to that later work.

CIARDI, JOHN. "The Researched Mistress," *Saturday Review* XL (March 23, 1957), 36-37. Moderates the opinions that *Homage* is a masterpiece. Criticizes the "literary" astmosphere of the poem, but concludes by comparing a passage in it to "the mad scenes in Lear."

"Congested Funeral: Berryman's New Dream Songs." Anon. review of *His Toy, His Dream, His Rest, Times Literary Supplement* (London), June 26, 1969, p. 680. Finds the volume to be clearer than *77 Dream Songs* and that, taken together, *The Dream Songs* have an "operative structure" of cross-references.

COTT, JONATHAN. "Theodore Roethke and John Berryman: TwoDream Poets," *On Contemporary Literature*, ed. Richard Kostelanetz. New York: Avon, 1964. Finds elements of Berryman's "twisting, elliptical

style" as early as *The Dispossessed*. Tends to summarize rather than
analyze.

DONADIO, STEPHEN. "Some Younger Poets in America," *Modern Occasions*, ed. Philip Rahv. New York: Farrar, Straus & Giroux, 1966. Traces the outlines of Beat and Academic poetry during the 1950's and 1960's; finds *77 Dream Songs* to be closer to Beat poetry.

ECKMAN, FREDERICK. "Moody's Ode: the Collapse of the Heroic," *University of Texas Studies in Endlish*, XXXVI (1957), 80-92. A comparison and contrast of William Vaughn Moody's "Ode in Time of Hesitation" (1900) and Berryman's "Boston Common." Concludes that Berryman's poem is more likely to survive.

ELLIOTT, GEORGE P. "Poetry Chronicle," *Hudson Review*, XVII (Autumn 1964), 457-59. Insists that one-third of the *77 Dream Songs* are incoherent; praises the "strange and exhilarating" effect of the style.

EVANS, ARTHUR AND CATHERINE, "Pieter Bruegel and John Berryman: Two Winter Landscapes," *Texas Studies in Language and Literature*, V (Autumn 1963), 309-18. Esthetical comparison of "Winter Landscape" and a Brueghel painting; strains to find meaningful analogues.

FITTS, DUDLEY, "Deep in the Unfriendly City," (New York) *Times Book Review*, June 20, 1948, p. 4. Review of *The Dispossessed;* finds in most of the poems "an aura of academic contrivance, a certain muzziness that is as hard to define as it is to ignore."

FITZGERALD, ROBERT. "Poetry and Perfection," *Sewanee Review*, LVI (1948), 690-93. Mixed review of *The Dispossessed;* praises the technique; has reservations about the Yeatsian ancestry and unevenness of some poems.

FRYE, NORTHROP. Review of *Poems, Canadian Forum*, XXII (October 1942), 220. Dislikes the "cultured liberal intellectual" tone of the poems; finds that they suffer from "hopeless complaint and constipated elegance."

GELPI, ALBERT. "Homage to Berryman's *Homage*," *Harvard Advocate*, CIII (Spring 1969), 14-17. Summarizes *Homage;* considers it and *The Dream Songs* "indubitable masterpieces."

GOLDMAN, MICHAEL. "Berryman: Without Impudence and Vanity," *Nation*, CCVIII (Feb. 24, 1969), 245-46. Confuses the composition dates of "The Nervous Songs," but notes in *His Toy, His Dream, His Rest* the presence of "certain obstinately recurring themes: Death, Fame and Love."

GREENE, GRAHAM. "The Badge of Courage," *New Statesman and Nation*, XLI (June 2, 1951), 627-28. Curt dismissal of *Stephen Crane* because of style and psychological bent.

HAMILTON, IAN. "John Berryman," *London Magazine,* IV (February 1965), 93-100. Distrusts Berryman's "gratuitous comedies of tone and syntax" that have been present throughout his career, a kind of "naughtiness" that reveals a self-contradiction in the poet's aims. Finds the style of *77 Dream Songs* to be "even more willfully corrupt" than that of *Homage.*

HOLDER, ALAN. "Anne Bradstreet Resurrected," *Concerning Poetry,* II (Spring 1969), 11-18. Juxtaposes details from *Homage* and from Helen Campbell's biography of Anne Bradstreet. Berryman has altered many details and thereby creates a "memorable woman," "more vivid and more moving than she ever is in her own writings."

HOWARD, JANE. "Whisky and Ink, Whisky and Ink," *Life* LXIII (July 21, 1967), 67-76. A valuable source of biographical and personal information about the poet. Superior to most critical articles in literary judgments and selective quotations.

JARRELL, RANDALL. Review of *The Dispossessed, Nation* CLXVII (July 17, 1948), pp. 80-81. Notes the Yeatsian influence; concludes Berryman was developing properly and would soon write better poems.

KELLY, RICHARD J. *John Berryman: A Checklist.* Foreword by William Meredith. Introduction by Michael Berryhill. Metuchen, N. J.: The Scarecrow Press, 1972. An indispensible aid to Berryman studies. Lists both primary and secondary materials. Contains a chronology and useful indexes.

KESSLER, JASCHA. "The Caged Sybil," *Saturday Review* LI (Dec. 14, 1968), pp. 34-35. *His Toy, His Dream, His Rest* is "quite obviously a masterpiece," and "infinitely quotable" because of its mixtures of styles.

KOBLER, J. F. Review of *His Toy, His Dream, His Rest,* (Dallas, Texas) *Times Herald,* March 16, 1969, Sec. F, p. 13. Praises individual Songs and their style—"a cross between James Joyce and Ezra Pound, a cross almost anyone can bear"—but finds volume weak in form.

KOSTELANETZ, RICHARD. "Conversation with Berryman," *Massachusetts Review,* XI (Winter 1970), 340-47. Berryman converses freely about his work; Kostelanetz observes the poet closely and summarizes Berryman's life.

KUNITZ, STANLEY. "No Middle Flight," *Poetry,* XC (July 1957), 244-49. Compares *Homage* to Hart Crane's *The Bridge;* finds the latter more successful. *Homage* "lacks inherent imaginative grandeur," and its language, borrowed from Hopkins, sometimes descends into "mechanical violence."

LIEBERMAN, LAURENCE. "The Expansional Poet: A Return to Personality," *Yale Review,* LVII (Winter 1968), 258-71. Unsuccessfully tries to distinguish between "expansional" and "confessional" poetry, but notes that the "accumulative effect of the *Dream Songs,* as well as the *Sonnets,* is overwhelmingly powerful."

"The Life of the Modern Poet." Anon. review of *Delusions, etc., Times Literary Supplement* (London), Feb. 23, 1973, pp. 193-95. A major review article that paraphrases a wealth of information about Berryman's career, but without documenting its sources.

LOWELL, ROBERT. "The Poetry of John Berryman," *New York Review of Books,* II (May 28, 1964), 3-4. Brief, perceptive survey of Berryman's career. Admits that "Henry's queer baby talk was at first insufferable," and criticizes *77 Dream Songs* for "mannerism" and incoherence; but concludes that "this great Pierrot's universe is more tearful and funny than we can easily bear."

MARTZ, WILLIAM J. John Berryman. University of Minnesota Pamphlets on American Writers, No. 85. Minneapolis: University of Minnesota Press, 1969. Fullest analysis of Berryman's work to date. Adjudges Berryman's poems to be "uneven"; *The Dream Songs* are a "distinguished achievement" but considered inferior to *Homage.*

MAZZOCCO, ROBERT. "Harlequin in Hell," *New York Review of Books,* VIII (June 29, 1967), 12-16. A major article that surveys Berryman's development. Prefers "The Dispossessed" to "Winter Landscape," *Homage* to the *Sonnets,* and *The Dream Songs* above all. Considers Berryman a "lesser talent" than Robert Lowell.

MEREDITH, WILLIAM. "A Bright Surviving Actual Scene: Berryman's *Sonnets,*" *Harvard Advocate,* CIII (Spring 1969), 19-22. Sensitive appraisal of the *Sonnets* as *tours de force* that present a "Racinian tale of conflict . . . between love and honor."

———. "Henry Tasting All the Secret Bits of Life: Berryman's Dream Songs," *Wisconsin Studies in Contemporary Literature,* VI (Winter-Spring 1965), 27-33. Compares *77 Dream Songs* to the best works of Lowell, Wilbur, and Roethke. Finds *77 Dream Songs* to be a "narrative" poem, "essentially humorous," and clearer than *Homage.*

MEYER, GERARD PREVIN. "Vigorous Swimmer in the Poetic Stream," *Saturday Review,* XXXI (July 10, 1948), 21. Enthusiastic review of *The Dispossessed.*

MILLS, RALPH J., JR. *Creation's Very Self: On the Personal Element in Recent American Poetry.* Fort Worth, Texas: Texas Christian University Press, 1969, pp. 28-32. Places Berryman among the "confessional" poets Robert Lowell, Sylvia Plath, and Anne Sexton.

NIMS, JOHN FREDERICK. "The Dispossessed," "World's Fair," and "The Traveler," *Poetry: A Critical Supplement* (April 1948), pp. 1-6.

Explication of the three poems with questions directed primarily to students.

OBERG, ARTHUR. "John Berryman: *The Dream Songs* and the Horror of Unlove," *University of Windsor Review,* VI (Fall 1970), 1-11. Adjudges the unifying theme of *The Dream Songs* to be "an unending expression of love" and of the need to be loved.

PORTERFIELD, JO R. "The Melding of a Man: Berryman, Henry, and the Ornery Mr Bones," *Southwest Review,* LVIII (Winter 1973), 30-46. Contains several inaccuracies of fact and interpretation, but clarifies "the Freudian implications of a suicide father for a near-adolescent boy."

ROSENTHAL, M. L. *The New Poets: American and British Poetry Since World War II.* New York: Oxford University Press, 1967. Places Berryman among the "confessional" poets; speculates that *77 Dream Songs* may have "signaled the end" of that movement. Prefers *Homage* to *77 Dream Songs.* Confident and superficial.

SEIDEL, FREDERICK. "Berryman's Dream Songs," *Poetry.* CV (Jan. 1965), 257-59. Finds "the unity of [*77 Dream Songs*] to be in the style alone," and the "humor [to be] wonderful."

SHAPIRO, KARL. "Major Poets of the Ex-English Language," (Chicago) *Tribune Book World,* Jan. 26, 1969, p. 4. Considers *The Dream Songs* "a major poetic work of our time"; denies that they are in the confessional mode. Compares Berryman to Chaucer in being able "to discover the language of his age and make it his own."

SLAVITT, DAVID R. "Deep Soundings and Surface Noises," (New York) *Herald Tribune Book Week,* May 10, 1964, p. 14. Almost totally negative review of *77 Dream Songs.* Humorous, interesting, and wrong-headed.

STEPANCHEV, STEPHEN. "Berryman's Sonnets," *New Leader,* L (May 22, 1967), 26-28. Feels that the *Sonnets* are "not as outstanding as the . . . *Dream Songs.*"

STITT, PETER A. "Berryman's Vein Profound," *Minnesota Review,* VII (1967), 356-59. Finds the *Sonnets* to be cerebral but concludes that Berryman "could soon be the greatest living American poet."

THOMPSON, JOHN. "An Alphabet of Poets," *New York Review of Books,* XI (Aug. 1, 1968), 34, 35, 36. Review article that makes perceptive guesses about the development of Berryman's style. Especially praises several poems in *His Thought Made Pockets & the Plane Buckt,* a volume virtually ignored by others (perhaps because of its lack of availability until it was reprinted in *Short Poems*).

"A Tortured Tryst." Anon. review of the *Sonnets, Times Literary Supplement* (London), July 4, 1968, p. 699. Finds Berryman's sonnets to be less satisfactory than George Meredith's; concludes that the *Sonnets* are simply exercises in technique.

TOYNBEE, PHILIP. "Berryman's Songs," *Encounter,* XXIV (March 1965), 76-78. Despite "an increasing obscurity in his later work," Berryman is placed alongside Lowell. Parodies the Dream Song stanza in an attempt to cast doubt on the originality of Berryman's style.

VENDLER, HELEN. "Savage, Rueful, Irrepressible Henry," *New York Times Book Review,* Nov. 3, 1968, pp. 1, 58-59. Briefly surveys the development of Berryman's colloquial style and finds its best expression to be in the "comic and tragic" *Dream Songs.*

WALSH, CHAD. "A Garland of Poets: Torrid, Elegant, Ascetic," (Chicago) *Tribune Book World,* Sept. 10, 1967, pp. 18, 22. The *Sonnets* are called "semi-juvenilia."

WASSERSTROM, WILLIAM. "Cagey John: Berryman as Medicine Man," *Centennial Review,* XII (Summer 1968), 334-54. Major article that explains the epigraphs to *77 Dream Songs* and traces sources to Olive Schreiner, Carl Wittke's *Tambo and Bones,* and Berryman's *Stephen Crane.*

WEBER, BROM. "Two American Men of Letters," *Western Review,* XVI (Summer 1952), 329-32. Finds *Stephen Crane* to be "primary in the history of criticism of American letters," "inspired," and apparently feels that the study is better than Crane deserves.

WILSON, EDMUND. "Stephen Crane—Hannah Whitall Smith," *New Yorker,* XXVI (Jan. 6, 1951), 77-85. Review; finds *Stephen Crane* to offer "brilliant insight" and to be "original and probing"; has reservations about the book's Freudianism.

"Zoo-Maze: The world in Vaudeville." Anon. review of *77 Dream Songs, Times Literary Supplement* (London), April 15, 1965, p. 292. Summarizes the "plot" of *77 Dream Songs;* explains many details and allusions.

Index